BUYING A GREAT BOAT

ARTHUR EDMUNDS

Editor: John P. O'Connor, Jr.

Bristol Fashion Publications
Harrisburg, Pennsylvania

Buying a Great Boat, by Arthur Edmunds

Published by Bristol Fashion Publications

Copyright © 2000 by Arthur Edmunds. All rights reserved.

No part of this book may be reproduced or used in any form or by any means-graphic, electronic, mechanical, including photocopying, recording, taping or information storage and retrieval systems-without written permission of the publisher.

BRISTOL FASHION PUBLICATIONS AND THE AUTHOR HAVE MADE EVERY EFFORT TO INSURE THE ACCURACY OF THE INFORMATION PROVIDED IN THIS BOOK BUT ASSUMES NO LIABILITY WHATSOEVER FOR SAID INFORMATION OR THE CONSEQUENCES OF USING THE INFORMATION PROVIDED IN THIS BOOK.

ISBN: 1-892216-35-3
LCCN: 00-131361

Contribution acknowledgments

Inside Graphics: By the author.
Cover Design: John P. Kaufman
Cover Photo: East Bay Yachts

Buying a Great Boat, by *Arthur Edmunds*

Buying a Great Boat, by Arthur Edmunds

Buying a Great Boat, by Arthur Edmunds

INTRODUCTION

When you go to a boat show or a dealer's showroom, there is an overwhelming number of boat types, styles, engines, and optional equipment. Clearly, you should be thinking about a definite type of boat before you proceed to look at the many available boats, either new or used. This choice should fit your personal preferences concerning the use of the boat and where it will be operated. It is true a small boat may be used for many different purposes, with the exception of providing sufficient accommodations for living aboard.

This book will show the differences in boat types and where each can be used efficiently. This will assist you in making a decision for the correct boat to fit your needs and enjoy the pleasures of being on the water. Surely, all of us would like to have a large boat with all the comforts of home, but most of us only have a few hours each weekend to enjoy floating on the water. A small boat under thirty feet in length may satisfy your requirements if you have little time to spend afloat. On the other hand, if you want to live on the boat, or take long cruises during your vacation time, a longer boat will provide those necessary arrangements and storage.

We are not only interested in the hull and interior, but the engine type is of prime importance as this is what gets us to our objective. Engine types and costs will be discussed and the advantages of each explained. Our own preferences largely determine what boat we will buy and each individual should find the most desirable boat described within these pages. I hope you will enjoy cruising as much as I have.

Arthur Edmunds

Buying a Great Boat, by Arthur Edmunds

Buying a Great Boat, by *Arthur Edmunds*

TABLE OF CONTENTS

INTRODUCTION   Page 7

CHAPTER ONE   Page 13
    SELECTING THE TYPE OF BOAT

    Types of boats and how they fit your personal needs.
    Ballasted and centerboard sailboats.
    Activities that are generally pursued on boats.
    Boats for calm water and boats for ocean use.
    Specialized boats: SCUBA, Water Skiing, Multihulls.
    Buying a used boat and choosing a bare hull.

CHAPTER TWO   Page 29
    BOAT DEVELOPMENT & ANCIENT HISTORY

    The building of boats in the past.
    The voyages of Thor Heyerdahl in his native rafts.
    Boats developed as iron fastenings came into use.
    Further development with engines instead of sails.
    Higher speeds demanded new hull shapes.
    Hydrofoils, hovercraft, and stepped hulls.

CHAPTER THREE   Page 37
    BOAT MATERIALS

    A description of boat hull construction in glass fiber, aluminum, steel and wood.

CHAPTER THREE cont.

The advantages and disadvantages of each material is discussed.

CHAPTER FOUR Page 45
ENGINES FOR BOATS

Discussion of torque at the propeller and the use of a reduction gear.

Gasoline and diesel engines are compared on the basis of fuel consumption, cost and weight.

Boat speed and the number of engines is selected for a particular boat weight.

Customary engine installations, water jets, and Surface Drives are discussed.

The total number of operating hours usually determines whether a gasoline or diesel engine is used.

CHAPTER FIVE Page 57
INSPECTING YOUR BOAT

Making a quick check of the hull, deck, and equipment.

The necessity of good anchoring gear and a boarding ladder or platform.

Check out the interior and the finish on the joinerwork.

CHAPTER SIX Page 73
PROFESSIONAL ADVICE

The necessity of hiring a surveyor and an engine mechanic both for your information and for your insurance company.

Checking the operation and accuracy of the electronics.

Making a run on a measured course to check boat speed.

CHAPTER SEVEN — Page 81
NECESSARY EQUIPMENT

What is considered safety gear and what else is desirable for comfortable boating.

How the area of operation affects the equipment requirements. Protected waters and the open ocean.

VHF radio communications and the electronics revolution.

Suggestions for safe boating.

CHAPTER EIGHT — Page 89
THE MOTIVATION FOR OWNING A BOAT

The time available for boating affects the type of hull that is selected as well as where it will be used.

Sometimes the like of older boats with traditional appearance influences the selection of a hull.

The pursuit of a sport may demand a special type of hull.

Sometimes the boat becomes a status symbol.

CHAPTER NINE — Page 95
SAILBOATS

A brief discussion of daysailers and cruising sailboats.

What type of hull is most suitable for ocean and for protected waters.

How the mast and rigging are put together.

CHAPTER TEN — Page 101
AN ANATOMY OF BOAT COSTS

A discussion of approximate new boat costs and the cost of components that fit inside the hull.

Replacement costs vary widely and some equipment

CHAPTER TEN cont.

that may be installed by a boat yard is analyzed.
    Bilge Pumps, Fathometers and thrusters are mentioned.

CHAPTER ELEVEN   Page 113
PROPELLERS

    Propellers are often discussed and are misunderstood.
    The basic function and method of operation are discussed.
    Diameter, Pitch and the number of blades are investigated.

CHAPTER TWELVE   Page 119
THE BOATING MARKET

    Doing business with a new boat dealer.
    When a used boat is considered, you may see a boat broker or check out a hull a friend wants to sell.

CHAPTER THIRTEEN   Page 123
SITUATIONS YOU WOULD RATHER FORGET

    A narrative of fourteen situations with which every owner should be familiar. Some were serious accidents and some were minor problems that are easily avoided.
Included are:

Loss of steering	Boat theft
Seaworthiness	Wrong alloys
Tanks at the stern	Excessive rolling
Opening portlights	Large ship dangers
Plumbing fittings	Aground

APPENDIX ONE   Page 141
LIST OF ILLUSTRATIONS

Buying a Great Boat, by Arthur Edmunds

APPENDIX TWO   Page 143
    INDEX

APPENDIX THREE   Page 149
    TOOLS & SUPPLIES

APPENDIX FOUR   Page 159
    GLOSSARY

ABOUT THE AUTHOR   ISBC

Buying a Great Boat, by Arthur Edmunds

Buying a Great Boat, by Arthur Edmunds

CHAPTER ONE
SELECTING THE TYPE OF BOAT

Your boat should be designed and selected for the type of activity you will be engaged, and the speed required. Keep these two requirements in mind whenever you look at a boat or when you have a discussion with friends who are knowledgeable.

In general, there are three types of boats: An open boat with no accommodations which may be used for fishing or water skiing; a semi-enclosed boat with minimum accommodations for two people; and a fully enclosed cruising hull for living aboard for a short period or permanently. See Figures 1, 2, and 3. Each of these three types may be designed with engines for any desired speed. All of the boat types may be used just for the enjoyment of being on the water in any cruising area.

Visualize the trips you will make and how much time you will be on the water. How many people will you be taking with you? Will you need sleeping and cooking facilities for overnight trips? Thorough planning before you buy a boat will insure purchasing the hull that will fill your needs and fit within your budget. Of course, a larger boat will provide more of the personal comforts, but it will be more expensive to buy and operate.

Sailboats are an entirely separate area of design and

have slow, displacement speed hulls favored by those who have a large amount of time to enjoy the quiet magic of sailing. Exceptions to this are the small sailboats that do not have ballast and are able to proceed at high speeds when the wind is aft of the beam. See Figure 4. Small, open, sailboats that do not have ballast require great care to prevent capsizing and it is only the skill of the crew that keeps them sailing at optimum speed and in the upright mode. For this reason, these open sailboats should only be used in protected waters.

One advantage of the small sailboat without ballast is it can be moved on a trailer to different sailing areas and provides a great deal of enjoyment. Your car probably has a towing weight limit and most states limit the width of a load on a trailer to eight feet. Be sure to keep these limits in mind when you plan to use a trailer. Of course, the mast and boom must be removed before placing the hull on the trailer.

Depending on the length of the sailboat, those with ballast may be fitted with an interior for long distance cruising and they are definitely the boats of choice for ocean crossings. Conversely, if you like to race sailboats, either in a class or with a handicap rating fleet, you may want to select the type of sailboat that fits in with your local group activities. The selection of a rig type for a sailboat is a matter of personal preference, but remember one mast is less expensive than two. For this reason, most sailboats are sloop rigged. For long distance cruising, some owners prefer a ketch rig as they can just furl the mainsail when the wind increases and proceed at optimum speed with a reasonable angle of heel.

Buying a Great Boat, by Arthur Edmunds

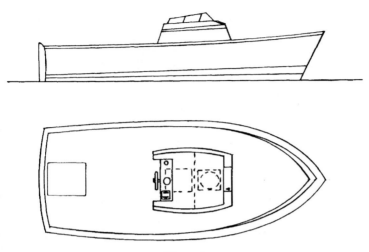

Figure 1
An open boat with head.

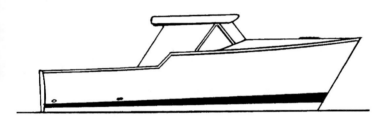

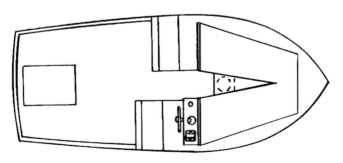

Figure 2
A cruising boat with berths and head.

Buying a Great Boat, by Arthur Edmunds

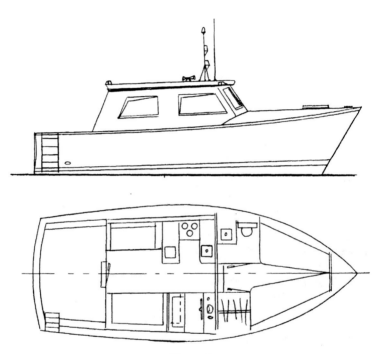

Figure 3
A semi-enclosed boat for overnight trips.

Buying a Great Boat, by Arthur Edmunds

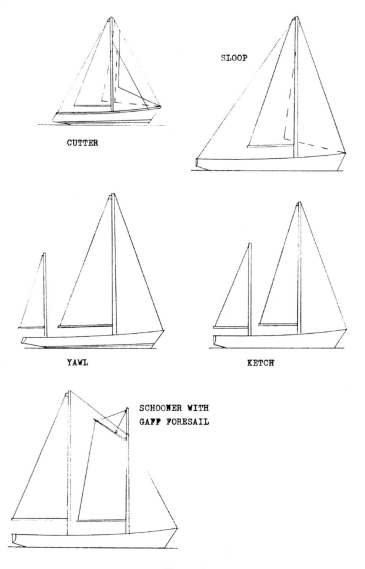

Figure 4

Buying a Great Boat, by Arthur Edmunds

SPECIFIC BOAT USE

You may want to consider the following activities to help in your selection of a boat:

Fishing in protected waters
High speed trips for ocean fishing
SCUBA diving
Water skiing
Day trips and swimming
Living aboard
Offshore cruising (Power & Sail)
Protected water cruising

There are many personal considerations that enter into boat selection. A thirty-foot boat may sell for sixty to one-hundred thousand dollars depending on engines and optional equipment. A forty-foot hull may be twice that amount. Primarily, you have to decide what your budget will allow, and cost is often the deciding factor in determining the size of the boat. Boat cost is discussed in a later chapter. You should decide where you are going to keep your boat and what additional monthly charges will be necessary. If a dock is in a shallow waterway, a deep draft boat may be out of the question. Deep keel, ballasted sailboats are often restricted to deep waterways with no bridges to slow access to the ocean.

The following will briefly describe boats for the above-mentioned uses. A fishing boat for protected waters is usually a small, open boat with the helm located in the center (center console) or at the bow so most of the deck area is open to walk around during the process of boarding a fish. If you are going well offshore to fish at the edge of the continental shelf, you will want a very different hull. In the ocean, the boat will usually have some portion of the forward half fully enclosed and watertight so water blown aboard will be deflected and the

Buying a Great Boat, by Arthur Edmunds

boat will not be swamped with sea water. Twin engines may be necessary to make the trip shorter and allow more time for fishing.

The deep 'V' (high deadrise) powerboat is probably best suited for travel in the rough water usually encountered when offshore fishing. The unusual word "deadrise" may require some explanation. When looking at the stern of a powerboat hull, the bottom, on both sides of the centerline, may be flat (zero deadrise) or have an angle to the horizontal. This angle to the horizontal is called deadrise and may be eight to twelve degrees in average hulls. When the angle is over twelve degrees, there is high deadrise which is best suited to rough water operation.

Offshore cruising across oceans usually calls for a ballasted sailboat with auxiliary engine power, but some rugged, trawler type yachts make long passages. These powerboats must have a large fuel capacity and usually choose the time of year with relatively calm waters. Recently, there have been some endurance races across oceans for both sailboats and powerboats. These demonstrations of strong hulls and a stronger crew have involved both monohulls and multihulls. Much can be learned from these efforts, but the average boat owner should not copy the itinerary.

Coastwise cruising, protected water cruising, and living aboard may be accomplished in either sailboats or powerboats over thirty feet with a comfortable interior and a well-built hull. There are many types of boats on the market that can be used for cruising, and your selection might well be based on the number of berths you require and the extent of the cooking facilities.

If you plan SCUBA diving, the aft deck of the boat you select should have a transom platform (swim platform) or a sloped ramp to provide easy access to the water. Secure storage for air bottles, regulators and wet suits must be installed. The forward half of the hull usually contains the helm, seating, galley and head. If you go diving for a few hours, a small, open boat can be used. Otherwise, the size of the boat determines the accommodations provided.

Water skiing is a specialized sport that requires a small, 35-knot, open boat with a very strong towing post at the stern. The helm is forward with an aft facing seat for an observer who keeps an eye on the person skiing. A few manufacturers produce a very special boat just for this sport and for the competition events held in various parts of the USA.

A small, open boat may be used for most activities in protected waters. The semi-enclosed hull is also fine for general boating, but lacks the facilities for living aboard. These two boat types are the most popular and are produced in large numbers by the many manufacturers. A fully enclosed cruising boat can be used for many purposes but is generally not used for high-speed trips and water skiing.

MULTIHULLS

One of the unusual hull shapes in boating is the multihull that was developed to improve both comfort and speed. Actually, multihulls originated with the South Pacific islanders for both rowing and sailing. They hollowed out logs to form the main hull and used smaller logs as outriggers to keep the main hull from tipping over. Small tree trunks with vine lashings were used athwart ships to hold the main hull and outriggers apart.

The catamaran is essentially two slender and identical hulls held together by two or more cross connecting beams. One or more decks may be constructed on these beams with extensive accommodations. Sailing catamarans may have centerboards and ballast but they are usually unballasted. The slender hulls result in minimum forward resistance and the wide spacing affords minimum rolling. Usually the beam of the catamaran is half the overall length of the boat.

Buying a Great Boat, by Arthur Edmunds

In day sailing and racing catamarans, the ratio of sail area to total boat weight is very high and high speeds can be expected, especially when the wind direction is aft of the beam. These light weight catamarans usually have hulls that are too narrow for accommodations, but cruising cats can have wider hull beam to enclose all the normal cruising amenities. Since the two hulls are separated, there is maximum privacy for the berthing areas. See Figure 5.

The primary advantage of the catamaran is the resistance to rolling and the wide beam available to spread out the arrangement. This great advantage has been put to excellent use with passenger ferries all over the world. There is no doubt catamarans will be used in greater numbers in the future. One of the few negative aspects of catamarans is the excellent property of wide beam becomes a detriment when looking for docking space at a marina. They usually have to dock at the outboard end of a pier with boats that are much longer.

Trimarans are essentially an outgrowth of the Polynesian proa, with the exception that two outboard hulls are used. These hulls limit the heel angle and are too narrow for good storage. The center hull is similar to a monohull and has all the accommodations. Usually there is no pilot house over the connecting beams, and thus the trimaran has fewer accommodations than the catamaran. Both types of multihulls can be used for powerboats or sailboats and clever design results in fine boats.

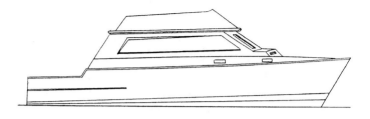

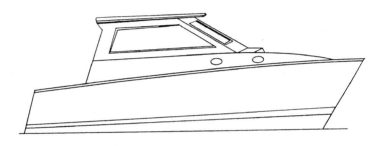

Figure 5
Profiles for a 56 foot and a 29 foot catamaran.

CONSIDER A USED BOAT

The market is usually flooded with used boats and there may be some good choices for those on a limited budget. As with any used product, the condition is most important in order to avoid any costly repairs. When you have located a used boat to fill your needs, it is imperative to have a professional surveyor inspect the boat both in and out of the water. From this report you can obtain estimates of the cost to put the boat in top condition. The engine is probably the most costly item on the boat, and the most important. It is money well spent to have a qualified mechanic run the engine and tell you what must be repaired for long term operation.

This professional advice is very necessary before

buying a used hull, and tells you about the condition of the particular hull. In addition, it is very informative to inquire of other owners about their problems with the make of boat. Boat brokers and boatyard managers are always a good source of information. Used boats may be located through friends, the newspaper, boating magazines, boat yards and boat brokers.

A used boat may be a very good selection for an owner who has time to work on the boat and who has good skills and tools. Trim pieces, shorted out electrical lamps, hull coverings, and plastic laminates are all within the capabilities of a patient handyperson. If the electronics are not working at the time the surveyor inspects the boat, it is probably best to subtract the replacement cost from the asking price. Modern electronic devices are fast becoming disposable products where it is less expensive to replace than repair. The cost of replacing various items in the boat is discussed in a later chapter.

BUILD A BOAT FROM A BARE HULL

Another alternative to the purchase of a new boat is the purchase of a bare glass fiber hull which will require the building of a deck and the interior arrangement. This is a large project and should only be undertaken by a hard worker who is willing to devote at least one thousand hours to the completion of the boat. It is usually more expensive to engage a custom builder to build a boat or to finish a bare hull and costs can be reduced substantially if the owner does a large portion of the work. This is detailed in "Building A Fiberglass Boat" by Arthur Edmunds, 1999, Bristol Fashion Publications, Enola PA, 1-800-478-7147.

It is sometimes difficult to find a bare hull, but they may be located by talking with boatyards, boat brokers, or designers. Powerboat hulls can usually be fitted out for any type of boat the owner may like, but the hull must be designed for the speeds you require. Powerboats should normally have a V-bottom as round bilge hulls are only efficient at low speeds. If a bare hull is under consideration, be sure to talk with other owners who have built from that particular hull so any problems may be avoided. See Figure 6.

The seller of a bare hull should provide proof the laminate is entirely made from alternating layers of glass fiber mat and glass fiber woven roving. An all mat laminate is not adequate as the strength of a glass fiber hull is determined by the woven roving. The mat is composed of short strands of glass fiber loosely held in a delicate sheet. The mat is available in various weights but 1.5 ounces per square foot is the most common. Woven roving consists of long fibers woven into a coarse, heavy fabric. 19 ounces per square yard is a common weight.

Laminates for a boat hull should never be made with the chopped glass fibers and resin that are sprayed from a chopper gun. These short strands are inherently weak and are only suitable for nonstructural parts such as shower enclosures and decorative panels. A conventional spray gun may be used, however, to put resin on the glass fiber material that has been laid in a mold. After the material has been wet with resin, it is rolled with a stainless steel disc roller to remove any entrapped air bubbles that would certainly weaken the resulting laminate.

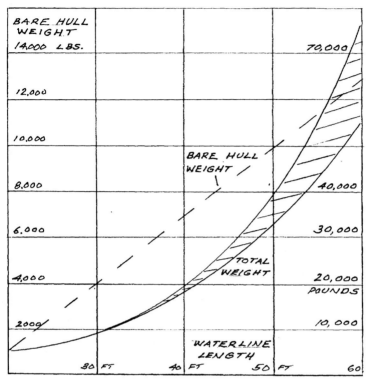

Figure 6

Buying a Great Boat, by Arthur Edmunds

Buying a Great Boat, by Arthur Edmunds

CHAPTER TWO
BOAT DEVELOPMENT & ANCIENT HISTORY

Primitive people carved the wood from the center of logs to make early canoes (or dugouts) and they tied logs together with vines to make rafts. In ancient times, the cloth was linen made from flax fibers, and sails were developed for the rafts. Paddles and oars were still the primary source of forward motion. In 1947, the Norwegian explorer, Thor Heyerdahl, built a balsa wood and bamboo raft (Kon Tiki) in South America and sailed it to the Polynesian Islands to show those islands could have been originally populated by people from South America.

In 1969, Heyerdahl conducted a similar sailing trip from Africa to the Caribbean to show how ancient people from Egypt could have brought their pyramid building skills to Central America. Although these trips were in the open ocean, they were made at the time of year when the seas were relatively calm. This reasonable selection of a sailing time was emphasized in the 1960's when a man from Miami, Florida sailed from the Canary Islands to the Caribbean to set a record for the smallest boat to make that ocean voyage. He sailed his eight-foot boat at a leisurely summertime pace.

As the need for larger, cargo carrying boats became evident, builders developed their talent to cut planks from logs, bend them by soaking in water, and hold them to frames with wooden pegs. The soft wood dowels were called tree nails or trunnels and they swelled when in the water to make a very tight fit. The planking was made watertight with tar, but the Vikings of Norway sometimes overlapped the planking edges to make a watertight seam (Lapstrake construction). The raft Kon Tiki and one of these Viking ships are on display in a maritime museum near Oslo, Norway. We can only guess at the voyages made from different countries, but there is a great amount of evidence to show ancient peoples recognized the need for strong, seaworthy boats and they used all the materials at their command to build better vessels.

Boatbuilders from different countries developed their own techniques for hulls and sails, but the common trend was towards larger, deeper and wider boats to carry more cargo. When iron became available, nails, straps and other forgings gained wide use on boats and the strength and seaworthiness was greatly improved. The fore-and-aft rigged sailing Dhow and Felucca became prevalent in the Red Sea and in the Mediterranean Sea as the limitations of the rectangular sail were realized. Even the latest, Twentieth Century square rigged sailing ships can only tack from port to starboard through 180 degrees on the compass. Modern jib-headed (Bermudan) rigged sailboats can tack through 90 degrees on the compass.

The ancient Dhow or Felucca usually had a short, rigid mast (solid tree trunk) that supported the middle of a lighter spar lashed to the top of the mast. The sail was lashed between the mast and spar. The spar was held at an angle to the mast by a line attached to the bottom of the spar. The lower end of the spar was moved from port to starboard as the boat was tacked. In some areas, the bottom of the spar was lashed permanently to the mast at deck level, and the sail lashed between the two. A line from the spar's upper end to the stern acted as the mainsheet.

The builder was the designer of early boats and the coastal countries of Europe and Asia saw the development of

Buying a Great Boat, by Arthur Edmunds

different types of boat hulls to suit fishing and coastwise travel. The bow and stern of early boats had pointed ends as the planks were bent to the centerline, and often they had carved figureheads at the top. The Chinese may have been the first to build a squared off stern with a deck house aft which was much higher than the bow. Possibly, they wanted to keep a following sea from breaking over the hull, or they needed room for the vertically sliding rudder they had invented. Early boats used a steering oar at the stern, and the rudder did not become popular until the twelfth century. A tiller was first used, and then steering ropes linked the rudder to the helm.

As more cargo weight was needed, the hulls became wider with more freeboard. This trend extended to the English and Spanish war ships that had at least two lower decks plus a gun deck and the main deck. The essentials of boat building and design remained virtually unchanged until the nineteenth century when steam ships were developed. From then until the present, boat design and construction has generally followed the progress of engine development, changing to meet the demand for larger and faster boat hulls.

Square rigged ships gradually disappeared from commercial sailing, especially in the USA, where lumber schooners and privateers were shown to be faster. They had all fore-and-aft sails, usually schooner rigged, with two or more masts, depending on their length. They were more efficient during most of their trips when the wind was forward of the beam. Many of these boats had a short spar, or gaff, at the top of the quadrilateral mainsail. This gaff held the top of the sail out from the mast and allowed more sail area at the upper portions where the wind is gustier than on deck. In addition, the shape of the sail can be changed by raising or lowering the gaff. The high weight of the gaff reduced stability and this gaff rig was replaced with simpler and lighter triangular sail (jib headed).

Buying a Great Boat, by Arthur Edmunds

MODERN BOAT DEVELOPMENT

As propulsion methods changed from sail to steam, and then to the internal combustion engine, boatbuilding also changed both in design and materials. Small boats continued to be made of wood planking until the 1960's, but the development of higher horsepower gasoline and diesel engines brought new hull forms to efficiently produce the higher speeds. Traditionally, boatbuilders made models of what they thought was an efficient hull shape. These small, wood models were towed in calm water to visualize the wakes and wave making resistance, and their dimensions were transferred to full-size patterns. Often, the hull lines were drawn on paper for later comparison with newer hull shapes. Drawings were seldom made for small boats as the builder was the designer and he personally supervised the construction crew during every stage of building.

Engineering principles were gradually applied to small boats and sophisticated test equipment was produced to measure the resistance of ship and boat models. These model tests show whether a new design is better or worse (has less resistance to motion) than the older design, whether power or sail. These model tests in a towing tank are very expensive and have to be conducted at a facility that has accumulated data for that type of hull. The scale of the model used is always a question among designers, but it is generally agreed that larger models produce more accurate results. The US Navy has used twenty- to thirty-foot models in their ship testing programs. These are towed in a long tank while resistance measurements are conducted.

Drawings of small boat hulls were not frequently made until the age of steam engines, but since that time we have an accurate record of all the changes as boatbuilders made progress in design and construction.

As the horsepower of marine engines made higher

speeds possible, designers experimented with hull shapes for faster boats. The traditional round bilge was found to be only efficient for slow speeds and the round at the bilge was replaced by a sharp corner (chine) and became known as the V-bottom boat. This hull form has taken over the entire boatbuilding industry, with the exception of displacement speed ships and sailboats. Unusual hull forms were tried by many designers and builders, but the V-bottom planing hull has remained very popular.

One of the unusual changes in hull formation is the stepped hull. This involves an actual step across the hull from port to starboard (athwartships) about four to nine inches deep. This is an attempt to have the hull run on as little hull bottom surface as possible, thus reducing frictional drag, at high speeds See Figure 7. To eliminate any possible partial vacuum forming at the step at very high speeds, a tube is usually installed from the step to the deck level.

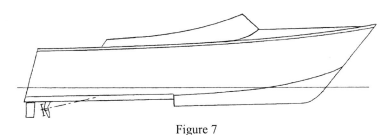

Figure 7

Since a stepped hull is only riding on a small area just forward of the step and at the stern, care must be taken to insure the total center of gravity of the boat's weight is located halfway between the areas on which the boat is riding. More than one step can be installed in the hull bottom but the hull is very sensitive to changes in trim, in both athwartships and fore-and-aft modes. It is not historically clear which was developed first, but the stepped hull principle is the same as the hull shape used in a seaplane bottom or floats. Good engineering ideas are often used in many different specialties.

Buying a Great Boat, by Arthur Edmunds

Hydrofoils have been tried since 1900 but it was fifty years before they came into commercial use as passenger ferries in Italy, Hong Kong, the Baltic countries, and on the Volga River. They are essentially monohulls with horsepower sufficient to produced at least fifty knots of speed. They have thin titanium, horizontal or inclined foils supported by struts extending below the hull. At high speed, the foils produce enough lift to support the weight of the boat with the hull completely above the water. With the hull resistance eliminated, the hydrodynamically shaped foils result in very fast trips, but they are usually confined to protected waters. In open ocean conditions, the foils may not stay in the water when meeting the trough of a wave and the boat is not supported during this momentary loss of lift. It is a fast, but expensive, method of traveling on the water.

Air cushion vehicles (ACV) are called hovercraft in England where they were developed. They are really more of an aircraft than a boat as they use aircraft type propellers to move forward, above the ground level. They are supported by a cushion of air that is formed by large fans directing air flow against the surface of water or ground. Once free of ground friction, the resistance to motion is greatly reduced, and high forward speeds are possible. The high cost of construction and operation has limited their use to commercial and military purposes.

Many different hull forms have been tried in the twentieth century in the quest for higher speeds and a more comfortable ride. We can't say one is better than the other, with the exception that some powerboats built for racing should only be used in calm water. Today, we see multihulls, both power and sail, charging across the ocean in search of record breaking history, but they do make these trips in the relatively calm summertime weather. It is not clear whether one hull form will eventually replace another, but probably each type will be further developed to produce better boats. The future emphasis on boat progress will probably be in the areas of greater boating safety and automation of engine maintenance, navigation, and anchoring.

Figure 6 notes the average weight of fully loaded boats and the weight of bare fiberglass hulls. Average boat weight (displacement) of recreational boats can be calculated by taking one-half of the cube of the designed waterline length (DWL) in feet. Boat weight varies greatly with the use of the hull. The same length hull can be used for a recreational boat or a commercial fisherman, possibly doubling the displacement.

Buying a Great Boat, by Arthur Edmunds

CHAPTER THREE
BOAT MATERIALS

GLASS FIBER

Most of the recreational boats built around the world are made with glass fiber, or a combination of glass fiber, aramid fiber, or carbon fiber. These are generally called plastic composite structures. The fibers are made with loosely arranged short fibers, woven fabric, and knit fabrics, or a combination of the three. The materials look similar to a coarse burlap in texture, although glass fiber is white, aramid fiber may be yellow, and carbon fiber is black.

These materials are saturated with a type of resin that forms a chemical bond with the fibers. The resin hardens by using a chemical additive and a hard sheet of plastic is formed with all of the strength provided by the encapsulated fibers. Layers of fabric and resin are laid on top of each other to achieve the required thickness. There are many different types of resins available for specific uses, including polyester, vinylester, and epoxy. Each forms a different chemical bond with the selected fibers and varied laminate strengths result.

When the fiber material is laid into a mold, it conforms to the shape of the mold surface. Almost any conceivable curvature can be made into a plastic composite laminate. The outside of boat hulls is coated with a special type of resin called a gel coat about one-sixteenth of an inch in thickness. This protects the laminate from the absorption of water and from the damaging effects of ultraviolet sun rays. The edges of the laminate at the sheer, and wherever a hole is cut for a through hull fitting, must be sealed with resin to prevent delamination from the entrance of water.

There is very little maintenance required on a glass fiber hull and this is the prime reason for the overwhelming acceptance of the material. Annual waxing of the exterior deck and hull is necessary to prevent fading and chalking of the gel coat. If there is a chip in the gel coat, or the hull becomes damaged from hitting the dock, repairs are easily made by the owner or by any qualified boatyard. Additional glass laminate over a hole in the hull is normally made with glass material and epoxy resin.

An average laminate weighs 96 pounds per cubic foot. See Figure 8.

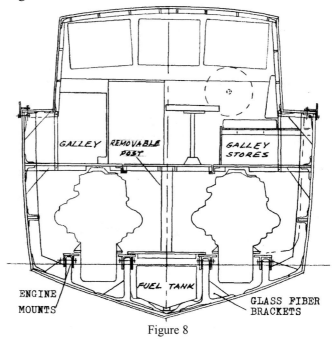

Figure 8

A section of a glass fiber hull.

Buying a Great Boat, by Arthur Edmunds

ALUMINUM

This lightweight metal can be made in various alloys and degrees of hardness. Only the alloys having a four number designation starting with 5 can be used for boat hulls as these alloys are not corroded by saltwater. For example, alloys 5052 and 5086 are most frequently used, and they are not heat treatable. Many structural and architectural shapes are made by aluminum extrusion and some carry the designation 6061 or 6063 which are commonly used and which are heat treatable. These extrusions can only be used inside the hull or above the main deck. Sailboat masts are sometimes extruded from 6061 alloy and they should be anodized, painted, or waxed to prevent long term corrosion.

Aluminum weighs 169 pounds per cubic foot and is very desirable for custom boats where light weight is an asset. There are some, aluminum boatbuilders that produce very fine boats, but most have concentrated on high speed commercial vessels. Many custom boats have aluminum superstructures above the main deck, even though the hull may be built of glass fiber, wood, or steel. This is done on some glass fiber custom hulls as the aluminum fabrication may be less expensive than the time consuming sanding of a custom glass structure. Aluminum deckhouses are used on wood or steel hulls to reduce the weight and maintain a lower center of gravity.

The proper alloy of aluminum produces good hulls with good saltwater corrosion resistance and the hulls do not have to be painted either inside or outside. But, both aluminum and steel are subject to electrochemical corrosion if there are stray electrical currents in the water from poorly wired shore power supplies. Both hull materials must have many zinc anodes and a meter to detect any hull voltage that may lead to corrosion of the aluminum. This problem only occurs around shore facilities and is usually not in evidence when underway.

The wholesalers who stock aluminum are usually cooperative in providing information on aluminum boats and Kaiser Aluminum in Oakland, CA has published an excellent book, *Aluminum Boats*, describing all the basic techniques of aluminum boat construction. The material cannot be overlooked when considering an entire boat or just a lightweight deck house.

STEEL BOATS

All ships and most small commercial vessels are steel as the cost of the material is lower than any other option. Welding is available in all ports of the world and repairs are easily made. Considering small craft, steel construction is normally too heavy unless the boat is a slow, displacement speed vessel. Tugboats and some fishing boats as small as fifty-feet are often built in steel, but yachts less than 130 feet long seldom are made from the material. Steel weighs 490 pounds per cubic foot, and is available in many alloys with different strength properties.

Maintenance problems with steel, both rusting and galvanic corrosion, are discouraging to the average boat owner, when they have seen rust streaks on some commercial hulls. If the paint coating has been scraped or chipped, the steel will definitely rust and people have received a bad impression from commercial boats that have only occasional care. Primarily, rust on steel hulls can be minimized when the hull is built by thorough cleaning and priming. In the high humidity of most builder's yards, a rust bloom will form on steel in a matter of minutes. The surfaces must be sand blasted or wire brushed over a small area at one time, and the primer coat must be applied immediately.

Steel can be bent, pressed, and formed into a slight compound curvature, but building a boat is much easier if the hull shape has lines that are conically developed, either on the drawing board or by computer program. The hull surface is part of the surface of a very large cone. To avoid cutting the sheet of steel into small triangles in order to conform to the compound curve lines, many commercial boats, and sailboats, are designed with a V-bottom (chine construction). Sometimes, two or more chines are used to make the hull shape closer to a round bilge. The surfaces between the sheer and the chine and between the chine and centerline keel are conically developed to make construction easier. This V-bottom shape does not detract from efficient operation, in fact, some builders insist on using chine construction.

Without a doubt, steel construction will continue to be a mainstay of shipbuilding. Builders worldwide regularly have schools to train a continuous supply of welders.

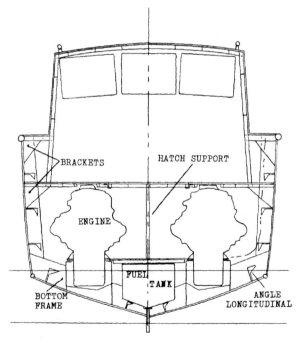

Figure 9

A section of an aluminum or steel hull.

Buying a Great Boat, by Arthur Edmunds

WOOD CONSTRUCTION

The traditional methods of wood boat construction are too time consuming to be used in volume production but wood boats are still popular with those who like the feel and smell of natural wood, and who plan to keep them for a lifetime. Wood requires much maintenance to keep water from soaking in and causing long term deterioration, both inside and outside the hull. Many of these problems can be avoided by covering the wood hull when the boat is built. The outside of the hull should be covered with glass fiber set in epoxy resin, and the same resin is used inside to thoroughly seal the wood. A construction section is shown in Figure 10.

There are some custom boats built today in the classic wood style, but most are built by owners who want to reduce costs by building their own hull. Frequently those builders use the strip plank method where almost square planks of wood are spliced together and then epoxy glued to the frames and to each other. In this manner, a lesser grade of wood can be used and labor is reduced as the planks do not have to be shaped (spiled) to fit the curvature of the hull. Only silicon bronze or stainless steel screws and bolts are used in boat hulls. Nails and staples are never installed. Strip planking also avoids the necessity of caulking the seams between planks and greatly reduces the required maintenance.

Other forms of wood construction have been used in various parts of the world with different degrees of success. One method that has been very popular with those building a very light weight hull for racing is cold molded construction. This uses many layers of thin wood veneers placed diagonally and athwartships over the hull and secured with epoxy glue.

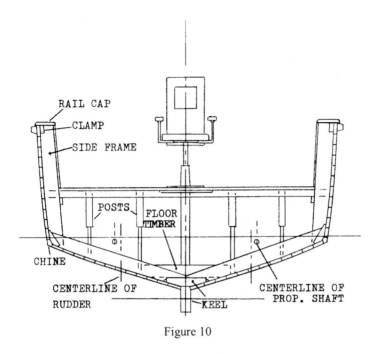

Figure 10

Section of a wooden hull.

SUMMARY OF BOAT MATERIALS

We really can't say any one particular boat material is any better than others. Large and small boats built of all the available materials have crossed the oceans and sailed around the world. We can use any material of varying thickness to meet any structural requirement. It is possible, however, to have a lightweight hull made of glass fiber or aluminum and still have the same total structural strength of a hull made from steel. When designing boat hulls we use an allowable material strength of 30,000 PSI (pounds per square inch) for steel, 18,000 PSI for aluminum, 14,500 PSI for glass fiber, and about 300 PSI for white oak, after applying a suitable factor of safety.

Buying a Great Boat, by Arthur Edmunds

Most builders of custom hulls concentrate on one particular material as they have found the most efficient assembly methods and have trained their personnel to work with that material. When considering a custom hull, it is wise to look at the hulls the builder has previously built.

Buying a Great Boat, by *Arthur Edmunds*

CHAPTER FOUR
ENGINES FOR BOATS

If you buy a new production boat it will probably have engines installed, but you can order a boat with your choice of engines. This assumes the fore and aft location is the same for which the hull was designed. We will briefly discuss each engine type and installation so you can make an intelligent choice for your particular mode of operation. First, let's define what we want the engine to accomplish.

Any engine converts the chemical energy of the fuel into mechanical energy to turn the propeller shaft. The measurement of the turning force on the shaft is called torque, and is defined in foot-pounds. Mathematically, torque equals engine horsepower multiplied by 5252 and divided by the rpm (revolutions per minute) of the shaft. ($T = 5252 \; HP/RPM$) We can see torque increases with higher horsepower and decreases with higher rpm. Most boats use a reduction gear in the same case as the reverse gear in order to reduce the engine rpm to an acceptable level, which increases the torque.

The propeller converts the torque of the shaft to thrust in order to move the boat. The larger the diameter of the propeller (more blade area in contact with the water), the more thrust it provides, consistent with maintaining the maximum engine rpm. One might reason that more torque is available with low shaft rpm and that more thrust is available with a large propeller diameter so this is what all boats should use. As with all design engineering, there are limits to what one can install. A large diameter propeller on a recreational boat would increase the draft to an unacceptable depth and the increased frictional drag would limit the speed on fast hulls. All good design is a compromise of objectives.

The engine only develops the maximum rated horsepower at the maximum rpm and thus the propeller must not be so large, both in diameter and pitch, that the maximum rated rpm is not attainable. In order to get a large amount of thrust in displacement speed (slow speed) boats, a large diameter propeller is desirable, and a slower shaft rpm is used. Ships may have a propeller rpm less than 100 and tug boats may have a propeller rotating at 300 rpm. Cruising powerboats may have a propeller rpm of 1200 and fast powerboats might have a shaft rotation of 2000 rpm. Each type of hull, engine, and method of operation has to be analyzed before selecting the correct reduction gear.

GASOLINE ENGINES

Engines burning gasoline are found in many types of installations; outboard motors, inboard engines driving outdrives and conventional inboard engines. Gasoline engines are basically lighter in weight and less expensive than diesel engines, but they do use more fuel per horsepower. Figure 11 shows the approximate fuel consumption for both gasoline and diesel engines. Fuel consumption can be estimated by dividing the horsepower by thirteen for gasoline engines and dividing by eighteen for diesel engines.

Generally, gas engines attain their horsepower at a higher rpm than diesel engines and thus are subject to more wear per operating hour. Automobile gas engines do very well over many years as they are usually run at half the maximum rpm with much time spent accelerating and decelerating between moderate speed and idle speed. The time spent on an interstate highway at high rpm is small when compared with the total operating hours. Therefore, the car gasoline engine operates in a far different manner than the same engine in a boat.

HORSEPOWER	GASOLINE	DIESEL
50	4	3
100	8	5.8
150	12	8.4
200	16	11.6
300	24	16.8
400	32	23
500	39	28
700	54	39
900	70	50

Figure 11

Estimated fuel consumption in gallons per hour at maximum revolutions per minute.

The engine in a boat is generally run at constant speed except when leaving or entering the dock. This constant speed is especially apparent when cruising or heading some distance offshore for fishing. Maintaining this relatively constant rpm is far different from the car operation and there is less wear on the internal parts if the required horsepower can be achieved at a lower rpm.

All engines should have freshwater in the cooling passages to prevent corrosion by saltwater. A heat exchanger is used with saltwater to cool the freshwater jacket. Of course, in freshwater there is no corrosion problem. Outboard motors, and the lower unit of an inboard/outboard installation are usually made of cast aluminum that has been treated to resist saltwater corrosion. When at the dock in saltwater, outboard motors and inboard/outboard installations should be tilted up out of the water. Flushing with freshwater is always recommended.

Outboard motors are desirable as the installation costs are reduced and replacement is much easier. Of all the boats sold in the USA, about one-third have outboard motors. With the engines exposed outside the hull, they are easy to work on, but are also easily stolen. Chains that secure the engine to the hull may prevent unauthorized removal. In many comparisons, outboard motors may be much less expensive to purchase than an equal horsepower inboard gasoline or diesel engine.

Gasoline inboard engines are sometimes adaptations of car engines and some are available to about 400 hp. These top performers are usually limited to light weight racing craft where maximum horsepower and rpm are used only for a short period of time. Higher horsepower is available and more than eight cylinders may be found, but at a very high price.

DIESEL ENGINES

Rudolph Diesel, developed and patented the engine in 1892. It has grown to be the most accepted type of engine in the world. Diesel engines for ships are built to almost any size and are rated at a certain horsepower per cylinder. Cylinders are then added to produce the desired power. Small diesel engines are used frequently, but fewer than four cylinders result in a great deal of shake, rattle, and roll, as seen in small cars or gensets with diesel engines. You can find an engine for most any application.

Diesel engines are widely used in Europe for both cars and boats as high taxes make diesel fuel more affordable. Most commercial boats use diesel engines for economy, safety, and durability. Diesel fuel is less flammable than gasoline and thus, safer. All engines require good maintenance, and diesels are no exception. With good care, diesel engines usually last for a large number of hours. Keep in mind, a recreational boat may only be used on weekends, for a total of about 250 hours each year, but a commercial craft may see 2000 hours per year.

Diesel engines are more expensive and are heavier than gasoline engines when compared with equal horsepower, but cruising boats shouldn't be concerned about a heavy hull. The cost of engines varies widely and may not include installation. Used engines are readily available and again the cost varies widely with the condition and whether the engine has been overhauled by a factory trained mechanic.

HORSEPOWER	NEW	USED
50	$9,000	$3000 - 4000
100	$13,000	$4000 - 6000
150	$17,000	$5000 - 9000
200	$21,000	$7000 - 11000
300	$29,000	$10000 - 17000
400	$37,000	$15000 - 23000
500	$46,000	$20000 - 30000

Figure 12

Approximate cost of one marine diesel engine in U.S. Dollars in 1999.

NUMBER OF ENGINES & LOCATION IN THE BOAT

Whether you have one or two engines is a matter of preference. Many owners feel two engines provide a factor of safety in case one fails, especially when going well off shore. In inland waters, you can usually find a tow from a sympathetic owner who hopes you will tow him if the situation is ever reversed. Some single engine boats also carry a small outboard motor for use if the primary engine fails. Single engine boats are harder to maneuver around the docks and the skipper who docks his single engine vessel surely shows everyone his excellent boat handling skills. A single engine reduces cost, weight, and maintenance.

Buying a Great Boat, by Arthur Edmunds

Many cargo ships and most sailboats have only one engine. Ships do this for reasons of economy, sailboats to reduce drag while under sail. Large powerboats that move at high speeds have two engines and the high costs associated with high speeds. Refer to Figure 13 for approximate boat speeds. If you like to be economical and have good boathandling skills, a single engine may be the proper choice.

HORSEPOWER	50	100	200	300	400	500	600
WEIGHT							
3,000	22	31	44	53	62	69	75
4,000	19	27	38	46	53	60	66
5,000	17	24	34	41	48	53	58
6,000	15	22	31	38	44	49	53
7,000	13	20	28	35	40	45	49
10,000	12	17	24	29	34	38	41
14,000	10	15	20	25	29	32	35
18,000	9	13	18	22	25	28	31
22,000	8.2	11.5	16	20	23	26	28
26,000	7.6	10.8	15	18	21	23	26
30,000	7	10	14	17	19	22	24

Figure 13

Approximate boat speed in knots for selected boat weights and horsepower. Weight is in pounds and the advertised horsepower is used.

Outboard motors and inboard/outdrive installations are necessarily at the stern of the boat, which keeps the remainder open for other activities. They also provide the desirable feature of having the fuel tanks toward the middle of the boat. This puts them closer to the center of buoyancy where there is little change of fore-and-aft trim from full to empty tanks. Having any tank at the stern is poor practice. When underway at half throttle, all powerboats should have only a small trim angle, with the bow about three degrees higher than the stern.

Buying a Great Boat, by Arthur Edmunds

CUSTOMARY INBOARD ENGINE INSTALLATIONS

Some inboard installations have the engine at the stern with the use of a V-drive. This has the engine reversed with the drive shaft at the forward end so the gears reverse the shaft direction and the tail shaft goes through the bottom of the hull in a normal manner. This type of installation is more expensive and it is used in larger custom powerboats and in some sailboats so the interior accommodations can be arranged to fit the owner's requirements. See Figure 14.

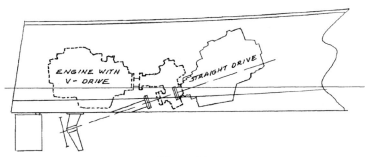

Figure 14

Straight and V-drive installations.

Actually, there are new products on the market that allow the inboard engine to be placed at any location in the boat. These are similar to the inboard/outdrive, which may be pictured as a 'Z' drive. The lower drive unit with the propeller goes through the hull bottom at any desired location, and the engine is directly coupled to the top of this drive. This type of installation has been used in sailboats for many years.

In many cases, the engineering of the type and location of engines is determined by the necessary interior arrangement.

Inboard engine installations try to keep the shaft angle

less than twelve degrees to the horizontal, in order to maintain propeller efficiency. This requirement puts the engine well forward of the stern and near the middle of the boat. In order to keep a watertight seal, there is a stuffing box on the shaft where it passes through the hull. Underwater, a bronze strut and rubber bearing support the shaft and propeller. The rudder is just aft of the propeller. In twin engine boats the rudders are usually set two inches off the shaft centerline so the shaft can be removed without removing the rudder. On single engine boats there may be a hole in the forward portion of the rudder for shaft removal.

Propellers normally have three blades on average powerboats, but hulls over forty-feet may use four blades for greater efficiency. Sailboats use two-bladed propellers to reduce drag while sailing, but may change to three blades when they face a long passage made under power. Your local propeller shop can assist with correct sizes for your engine and reduction gear, but it is generally true a large diameter is more efficient, if other factors are considered. This diameter selection must allow a space between the propeller top and the hull (tip clearance) of at least twenty percent of the propeller diameter. For example, a 30-inch diameter propeller should have six inches between the tip of the propeller and the hull.

OTHER PROPULSION METHODS

SURFACE DRIVES

Manufacturers offer a surface drive system where the engine may be located in any part of the hull. The drive shaft penetrates the transom (at the stern) and not through the bottom of the hull. Aft of the transom, the shaft and propeller are positioned with two hydraulic cylinders so the top of the propeller is just below the surface of the water. The special propeller is designed for high-speed operation and approximately twenty percent greater speeds are possible with the same horsepower. Steering is accomplished by moving the outboard shaft left and right with the hydraulic cylinder. A rudder is not used.

The surface drive system has higher efficiency as there is lower frictional drag from the lack of any appendages below the hull. Since the shaft, strut, and rudder are not projecting from the bottom of the hull, the water flow is smoother and is not interrupted by this hardware. This system does produce a large propeller wake at high speeds and does not offer any slow speed advantages except unusually shallow draft. This system was invented and patented by Howard Arneson and has proven to be very popular for high-speed, shallow draft boats.

WATER JET DRIVE

Another system that provides very shallow draft is the water jet. This uses an opening in the bottom of the hull to take water into a duct that encloses a specially designed propeller. This duct bends aft so it exits the hull at the transom just above the waterline. The propeller moves the water aft at high velocity and the reaction moves the boat ahead at high speed. To reverse, a door is hinged down over the exit opening and the water flow is deflected forward. This reaction moves the boat aft. Steering is accomplished by hydraulic cylinders moving a deflector plate in the water jet stream.

A conventional inboard engine, or a gas turbine, turns the propeller for fast operation without gear installed below the hull. All of this is achieved at high initial cost in both the purchase and installation of the water jet casing. These water jet drives have been used successfully in all types and lengths of fast boats for many years. They gained popularity in the USA after being used in the US Navy thirty foot patrol boats during the Vietnam War. The small jet ski boats (personal watercraft) use water jet drives to avoid the possibility of a person being injured on a propeller. If a boat is not frequently used, you may get barnacles and marine growth in saltwater on the water intake duct surface, which may be hard to remove. For shallow draft operation, this is a popular system.

SUMMARY OF ENGINE SELECTION

If you want a very economical boat, it may be suitable to have a single outboard motor in a boat under thirty feet and a single inboard engine in a larger boat. It is also practical to select an engine your local mechanic is accustomed to servicing. Don't buy an engine that will require parts from another part of the world. If you can do minor maintenance on the engine, it is always necessary to have water pump impellers, oil filters, fuel filters, and tools on board.

Figure 15 shows the equipment in the engineroom of a cruising boat. Smaller boats, and those intended for just an afternoon ride will not have the luxury of hot water, an A.C. generator, air conditioning and a watermaker. Each owner, and their budget, must determine what is necessary and what is optional for the intended area and type of operation. If the boat will be used for a large number of hours, it may be a good investment to buy a diesel engine so fuel costs may be reduced. This is the reason most commercial boats have diesel engines.

Whatever the engine and type of installation, it is always desirable to have a keel on the bottom of the hull a few inches lower than the bottom of the propeller. The keel will protect the propeller when in shallow water, and will allow the boat to follow a straighter course, especially in rough water and when using an autopilot. In addition, the propeller shaft strut on two-engine installations should be in the shape of a Y so the lower arm provides some protection for the propeller.

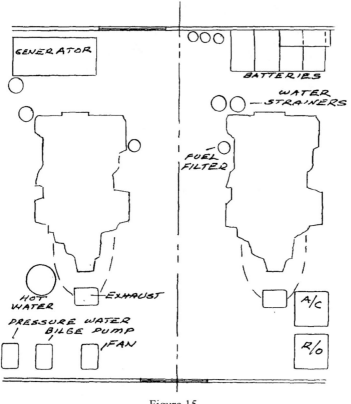

Figure 15

Typical engineroom plan. A/C is air conditioning compressor and R/O is reverse osmosis watermaker.

Buying a Great Boat, by Arthur Edmunds

CHAPTER FIVE
INSPECTING YOUR BOAT

The quality of manufactured boats is usually very good, although errors and oversights will happen. In any business there are always a few, small operations that have not heard of the term, Quality Control. It is always necessary to look at every boat with great care, not overlooking any detail. Responsible builders will have good warranty programs and will usually attend to problems that surface after delivery. Flaws that affect safe operation are reported to the U.S. Coast Guard who require builders to make repairs and changes on all hulls that have been produced. Your boat will have a Hull Identification Number (HIN) molded into the top of the transom (stern). It has letters denoting the manufacturer, the number of the hull, and the model year.

Like any other product, we assume the boat has been well made, but mistakes can happen when a worker quits for the day and forgets a procedure when returning to the job after a long weekend. I will outline some important points to look at before deciding on a particular boat. A boat dealer who tries to influence you into not inspecting the boat is certainly not the dealer who should get your business.

HULL

The bottom of the boat is usually covered with an Antifouling coating that makes it difficult to see the hull surface. However, it can be inspected using the same methods as the portion above the waterline. The exterior gel coat on a glass fiber hull should have a smooth, glossy finish that reflects like a mirror. Small, slightly raised blisters may develop in some areas, and these must be repaired in order to preserve the integrity of the laminate. These blisters normally occur below the waterline and may allow water entry which would result in serious delamination. These blisters are formed by improper materials or by poor laminating procedures. Also, delamination will occur from water entry if through hull fittings are not properly sealed.

Look over the entire hull for any scratches or gouges where the hull has come into contact with the dock or anchor. These can be filled with gel coat or epoxy glue and buffed to a smooth finish.

The line denoting the attachment of the deck to the hull is called the deck to hull joint. It must be sealed with caulking and bolted to form an extremely strong structure. Some configurations of this joint are shown in Figure 16. A very important part of this assembly is the rub rail which must project at least two to four inches from the hull surface for adequate protection when hitting the dock. This rub rail may be made from a plastic extrusion, an aluminum extrusion, or wood. It must be bolted through the hull.

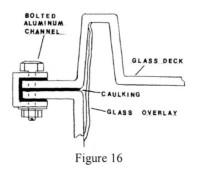

Figure 16

Typical deck joint.

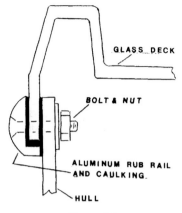

Figure 16a

Typical deck joint.

Since the hull laminate has a gel coating on the exterior, it is difficult to inspect the laminate for any possible problems. The interior of the hull can be checked, however, if it is not painted. Light colored, almost white, areas of the glass laminate show where resin has not saturated the glass fibers and where the layers of glass laminate have not adhered to each other. This is a serious situation that allows the layers to flex independently as they are stressed when the hull moves through the water. This condition is called delamination, which may lead to hull failure if not repaired. The repair is made by drilling small, shallow holes into the laminate into which epoxy glue is injected with a glue syringe.

Assuming the boat is out of the water, move the propeller up and down on an outboard motor or inboard/outboard installation. Any excess movement shows wear on the propeller lower shaft bearings. On an inboard engine installation, try to move the propeller shaft up and down at the shaft strut. This checks for excessive wear on the rubber bearing inside the strut. The propeller should be without nicks or bent blades. A bronze propeller should not have any pits or spots that appear to be pink in color. This is an indication of galvanic corrosion when the zinc is removed from the bronze alloy of copper, tin, and zinc. Stray electrical currents in the water cause this type of corrosion. Blocks of zinc attached to the shaft strut may decrease this corrosion.

If the boat has a keel, look for any cracks or dips in the bottom surface, especially where the hull is resting on blocks. These may be an indication of insufficient laminate thickness in the keel. The bottom of the keel -- or boat hull on centerline if there isn't a keel -- should be a half inch in thickness on boats under thirty feet, three quarter of an inch on boats thirty to thirty-five feet, and one inch in thickness on hulls thirty-five to forty feet in length. It is almost impossible to physically check this thickness without drilling a hole, which no one wants to do. But the thickness can be checked with an ultrasonic thickness tester. Some cruising boats have used epoxy glue or a polysulphide adhesive compound to attach a wood wear strip on a glass fiber hull. This prevents nicks in a glass keel when going aground.

A glass fiber hull will flex when a boat pounds into a seaway, and excessive flexing may lead to cracks. This is prevented by installing glass fiber framing on the inside of the hull. These frames are necessary in all boats, with all materials, and are spaced twenty to thirty inches apart. Check the hull interior to see these frames are in place and are secured to the hull with glass overlay, in a glass fiber hull. They may be installed either transversely or longitudinally. The bulkheads also act as framing to stiffen the hull and they also must be overlaid with glass material on both sides.

DECK

Before you buy a boat, you want to be sure of the installed hardware and equipment on board so you know what may be necessary to purchase to meet your individual requirements. Your inspection must note the gear as well as any obvious repairs that are needed. The deck should have a good appearance as well as a nonskid surface to prevent injury. At least six chocks and cleats (three of each on one side) should be available for proper docking. On boats under thirty feet, the cleats can be eight inches long for use with three-eighth inch line, but over thirty feet, they should be twelve inches long to allow at least two turns of half-inch diameter or larger line.

It is important to have storage space on deck for dock lines, fenders, and life jackets (PFD). On a sailboat, these may be in a cockpit seat locker or in the lazarette.

FLEXING

Large areas of the deck must be adequately supported by deck beams in order to prevent excessive flexing. When you step on a large deck area, and you can feel it flex, you know that deck beams should be installed. This deck flexing can be dangerous as an unexpected deck movement can cause a person to lose balance and fall. Life lines must be installed all around the deck edge to keep the crew from falling overboard. They are supported by stainless steel pipe stanchions at least thirty inches in height. These stanchions, and all hardware, must be through bolted to the deck with three or four bolts, nuts, and lock washers. Under the deck, an aluminum backing plate is used around the bolts to evenly distribute the load.

ANCHORS

Every boat must have an anchor and line to use when you stop for lunch, fishing, or SCUBA diving. When an engine fails, the anchor becomes a vital necessity to keep the boat from drifting out to sea or onto the rocks. I was put into an emergency situation the first time I docked a three hundred foot ship. The ship was about eight hundred feet from the dock when there was a complete loss of electrical power, including the engineroom telegraph communications. The sound powered phones were jammed with ten people trying to communicate. The only recourse was to anchor the ship until the emergency could be cleared.

A small boat will usually have mechanical or hydraulic engine controls, but this same emergency could possibly happen, and the anchor should be ready to use. When cruising, two anchors are always recommended.

The minimum anchor weight is ten pounds for a boat under thirty feet, twenty pounds for a boat between thirty and thirty-five feet and thirty pounds for a boat between thirty-five and forty feet. The anchor line can be Nylon of the same diameter as the dock lines: three-eighths of an inch in diameter on boats under thirty feet, half inch diameter on boats between thirty and thirty-five feet, and five-eighths inch diameter for boats between thirty-five and forty feet in length. Make sure the end of the line is tied or cleated to the boat so it will not be lost while anchoring. A platform with a roller at the bow is installed on many boats to prevent the anchor from banging into the hull. Ten to twenty feet of anchor chain is recommended for boats over thirty feet in order to keep the pull on the anchor more parallel to the contour of the bottom. Always check your anchored position frequently to make sure the anchor has not slid over the bottom.

Anchor windlasses are useful for both raising the anchor and for bringing the boat closer to the dock with the lines when a strong wind is blowing the boat farther away. Windlasses are not usually necessary in a boat under thirty-five feet in length. When the anchor is snagged on the bottom and will not break loose, it can sometimes be retrieved by running the boat under power towards the anchor until the line is vertical. The anchor line is then cleated and the boat run ahead under power. Repeating this on different headings usually releases the anchor from the bottom. If not, the power of the anchor windlass may be used to maintain a constant strain on the anchor line while the boat engine is reversed under full power. Anchoring is a true test of good seamanship.

Anchor windlasses are manufactured in many sizes and can be manual, electric or hydraulic. They are denoted by their pulling force on the line, which should be at least five hundred pounds for a boat thirty to thirty-five feet in length, and eight hundred pounds on a boat thirty-five to forty feet in length. A manual windlass should have a mechanical advantage of at least twenty to one. This means that a six hundred pound force will pull on the line if you push the handle with a thirty pound effort.

Electric winches can be A.C. or D.C. powered. Alternating current is preferable if there is a generator to supply the power. A one horsepower motor may drive a windlass with an eight hundred pound line pull. It would use about sixty-two amperes of current with a 12 V.D.C. system. It may be better to use a twenty-four volt system to reduce current requirements and to locate the batteries just below the windlass. They would be charged, when the boat is at the dock. If the windlass used battery power located in the engineroom, the long wire run would result in a drop in voltage and very large diameter, expensive cables.

CLIMBING ABOARD

When swimming, it is hard to climb back aboard over the high hull sides, even on a boat under twenty-five feet. Flexible ladders are not much help as the steps are pushed under the bottom of the boat when you step on them. Molded steps are good, but you still have to pull yourself up to the lowest step. Some manufactured boarding ladders are double hinged and are usually located at the stern. The rigid lower section provides a strong lower step in the water. The importance of the boarding ladder cannot be overemphasized as a necessary safety feature.

It is always preferable to have a swim platform permanently installed at the stern. Swimmers and SCUBA divers can then get a leg on the platform, about six inches above the water, and roll onto the surface. In the worst situation when a person is rescued after ingesting too much water, it is much easier to pull them onto the swim platform rather than trying to pull them up and over the hull side.

INTERIOR

When you first look at the inside of the boat you are considering for purchase, try to visualize your family or crew living aboard overnight. Do you have sufficient privacy with the berthing arrangement? Is the galley adequate for preparing limited meals? Of course, if you are looking at a boat just for day use, the interior will not present a problem. An insulated ice chest for sandwiches and cold sodas is always a good solution for short trips.

WATER LEAKS

Look around the interior below the deck and portlights. Dark streaks show there is a water leak and a repair is required. If the overhead (underside of the deck) and the hull sides are covered with outdoor carpeting or other material, look for loose material and spots that indicate water leaking. There shouldn't be any water accumulation in the bilges of a glass fiber boat unless there are leaks and you should lift the floor hatches to check for any problems. Mistakes do happen.

Most boats have berths at the bow, which may be molded of glass fiber or built of plywood and painted. Particle board or flakeboard should never be used on a boat as they absorb moisture and come apart over a period of time. Also, nails and staples are never used on a boat of good quality. The volume of space forward of the berths should be watertight up to the berth height. This is the area most frequently involved in a collision with a dock, boat, or rocks, and any crack in the laminate may allow water to enter. A watertight compartment will prevent flooding the remainder of the hull. The interior floor (cabin sole) should be securely overlaid with glass to the hull and it should have floor hatches so every part of the bilge may be inspected.

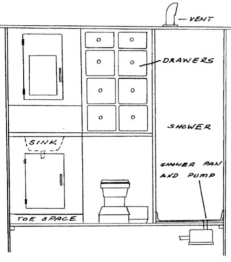

Figure 17

Typical head arrangement.

THE HEAD

You probably spend the least amount of time in the head, but it must be carefully arranged for convenient use and with some degree of comfort. Even small boats with an open deck and no cooking or sleeping facilities may have a toilet room with just sufficient headroom for sitting. There should be at least twenty-four inches of width at the toilet and a shower space must have at least twenty-four inches as a minimum dimension. Preferably, a shower should be thirty-two inches square. A small drawer for each person is a convenient space for toilet articles as well as one or two drawers for first aid supplies. A water trap type of ventilator over the shower is a true necessity. Figure 17 shows the arrangement of a head in a cruising boat.

THE GALLEY

Cruising boats have cooking facilities that can range from a two-burner alcohol stove and ice chest to an all electric galley, just like home, if there is a generator on board. The range (cooker) can be fueled with alcohol, compressed natural gas (CNG), or propane (LPG). When using gas as a fuel, the bottles must be stored on deck, outside the deck house, with a shut off valve in the gas line. If on a sailboat, the range must be gimballed athwartships so the range remains level as the boat heels with the wind. There are several safety concerns which should be investigated thoroughly, when using CNG or LPG.

Refrigeration is probably the main concern in a galley as we all prefer cold drinks, fresh rather than canned vegetables, and frozen foods of all types. Eating aboard a boat is always much simpler without refrigeration. Without an installed generator, there is a choice of an ice chest, mechanical refrigeration run from a belt driven compressor mounted on the main engine, or the short term option of using holdover plates inside a household electric refrigerator. This electric refrigerator operates at the dock and the frozen plates keep the contents cold for a few hours while underway. Whatever the system, you should operate the refrigeration to make sure it produces a cold box before buying. refrigeration systems may cost several thousand dollars to replace.

If you have a built-in ice chest, there should be four to

six inches of urethane foam insulation on all sides, outside of a glass fiber, or molded plastic watertight box. There should be a removable shelf to keep the food away from the wet ice. It is best to remove water from the chest with a pan and sponge. If there is a water drain to the bilges, food particles will accumulate in the bilge and cause a foul odor. The opening should be about twenty-four inches square on the top. Figure 18 shows a typical galley.

The area in and around the galley is packed with drawers, shelves and cabinets in every available space. Just as in the kitchen at home, you can never have enough storage space for all the utensils and canned foods. Shelves for dishes should have partitions to keep them from banging around with the roll of the boat. Plastic cups should be used for drinks and food should not be bought in glass containers whenever possible. Two stainless steel sinks are always better than one.

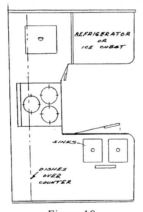

Figure 18

Typical galley arrangement.

TYPE OF FINISH

You want to have a good looking interior and one that is easy to keep clean. This can be accomplished by a careful selection of finishing materials, and the use of light shades of color, except for the flooring, which may be dark. Generally, the following are the options for the boat's interior finish:

1. Cover with an outdoor carpet.
2. Prime and paint. The edges may be a shaped wood molding, a plastic laminate, or a plastic 'U' shaped molding.
3. Cover with a plastic laminate.
4. Use pre-finished plywood for all bulkheads and joinerwork.
5. Sand, seal, and varnish if the underlying plywood has an acceptable finish. This must be renewed every few years.
6. Cover with a textured, vinyl wall covering.
7. Install fine wood paneling, an expensive alternative.

Figure 19

Fine wood finish of a sailboat interior.

Figure 19 shows a good looking sailboat interior that uses pre-finished plywood and varnished wood moldings. The corners of the bulkheads and joinerwork should be rounded to avoid bruises when the boat rolls and people lean into the corners. The overhead (underside of the deck) and sides of the hull are often covered with outdoor carpeting by many manufacturers, as an alternative to painting. An expensive option would be to glass wood furring strips to the glass laminate. Many types of decorative panels, in any material, may then be screwed to the wood strips. Electric wiring should be located so it can be easily repaired.

The cabin sole may be molded glass fiber with a nonskid finish. Often, this molding is extended upwards to form a foundation for the interior joinerwork. The sole may also be made from decorative, pre-finished plywood, and outdoor carpeting may be used. Whatever the construction, there should be hatches to all parts of the bilge.

THE ENGINEROOM

If you are not mechanically inclined, and don't like to check the minor points on you car engine, you may be amazed at the amount of complicated equipment located in a boat's engineroom. It is important, however, to look at a few important points when you first see the boat. The oil dipstick and coolant water fill cap must be within easy reach. The propeller shaft stuffing box (packing gland) keeps water from entering the hull and it should be easily reached for tightening. The hot cooling water is normally injected into the hot exhaust gasses in a cast iron fitting sometimes called an exhaust elbow. This cast iron corrodes quickly due to the sulfur in the exhaust forming sulfuric acid. These fittings should be checked annually as well as all of the exhaust lines.

Whenever there is a hole in the hull for installation of a drain or cooling water inlet, the bronze through hull fitting must have a bronze valve (seacock). this will allow you to close the opening when an emergency occurs, or when repairs are made to the piping. Check these valves semi-annually to make sure they work easily. The sea water piping to the engine, or other equipment, should have a filter in the line to keep weeds out. This filter cannot be assembled with reducing elbows to match the pipe sizes as the elbows will trap weeds and stop the water flow. Reducing pipe fittings should only be used in straight sections of piping. If a permanent fire extinguishing system is not installed, it is highly recommended that a portable extinguisher be located near the engineroom door.

Other equipment in the engineroom may include a generator for complete electric power, a watermaker for use on long trips, air conditioning, hot water heater, a pressure water pump, and shore power wiring. You may not need all of this if you plan only trips for a few hours, but whatever is installed, it should be checked for proper operation before buying. You should be able to charge all of the batteries on the boat both when the engine is running and when on shore power from the dock. Charging systems are readily available from reliable marine stores. Never get close to the engine when it is running, and especially keep clear of the propeller shaft and coupling while in operation. If you have to check the water or oil levels when the engine is running, make sure you only touch the equipment with one hand, and keep trouser bottoms away from the equipment.

All compartments of the hull (between bulkheads) should have a bilge pump in case of accident or water entry. These are submersible pumps with float switches and an alarm at the helm station shows when these pumps are operating. When a pump runs continuously, the alarm tells the owner when immediate action is required. The most common cause of excess water in the hull is when a hose clamp loosens. All piping connections should have two hose clamps. Electrical wiring should be supported with plastic clips and located above the waterline, all around the hull.

WINDOWS AND VENTILATION

Certainly, there should be good visibility from the helm, all around the horizon. In order to better see boats that have the right of way, the helm must be located on the boat's centerline, or to starboard. At least one section of the windshield should open to allow good ventilation. All windows should have drains so water does not collect at the bottom sill. Usually, the lower window frame is sloped down and outboard so there is a positive drain. Most owners like the steering station to be covered, or located inside the deck house, to keep out the cold, rain, and sun.

It is important to have good air circulation inside the boat. On a cruise, the air can become very stale and the crew will develop headaches if there are not sufficient air intakes. In any humid climate, mildew will grow rapidly on most surfaces if the air is not circulated. When underway, hatches can be opened and the interior becomes pleasant. But, we are mostly concerned with the eighty percent of a boat's life that is spent at the dock.

There are many water trap type of ventilators on the market that are mounted on deck, the cabin top, or on a hatch. They are a vital part of enjoying boating as any experienced owner will testify. Unfortunately, they are usually ignored by manufacturers and you will not see them in the glossy magazine advertisements. Probably, they don't want to add to the cost of a boat and they wrongly assume the boat will be operated in a cool climate or have the air conditioning running. Locate these vents over the showers, the passageways, and over the galley range.

It is poor practice to have opening portlights in the hull sides below the sheer. Someone is always leaving one open and unusual waves from other boats have a way of entering your boat when you least expect it. Air circulation should be provided from vents on deck and not from opening portlights. We know of one motor yacht that ran aground and heeled over about seventy degrees. Water entered portlights that were located low on the hull side and the boat sank with one side on the bottom. A fortune was spent in re-floating and rebuilding the boat. The portlights were then welded shut, after the damage had been done.

Good air circulation is a necessity in the engineroom both for good fuel combustion and to keep the temperature of the space below a hundred degrees. If the engine does not get sufficient air for combustion, the engines are operated at less than designed horsepower and the owner wonders why his boat is so much slower than another with the same engines. If an engine space is still very hot after the engines have not been used for ten hours, it is a sure sign there isn't enough air circulation, and additional air ducts should be installed.

The air supply to the engine should come from outside the deck house, or outside the engine space on a small boat, preferably above the sheer. Air intakes in the hull side below the sheer are poor practice. There have been many cases of low freeboard sportfishermen trolling in the trough of a wave and rolling to the point where water enters the hull side air vent. The minimum air vent opening on each side of the hull, in square inches, is one third the total engine horsepower. For example, if there are two, three hundred horsepower engines, the minimum air vent opening is two hundred square inches. A ten inch by twenty inch opening in the cabin side is not excessive in appearance. A duct takes the air below to the engineroom, which can be concealed under a seat.

Natural air circulation is good, but a continuous duty fan is much better. The capacity of this fan should be three times the total installed horsepower, in cubic feet per minute. It is good to have a smaller exhaust fan installed in the aft bulkhead of any engineroom. This is used for an hour or two to remove engine heat after the engine has been secured for the day. A fan and duct to the main deck can be used but do not use the intake fan in place of an exhaust fan.

Buying a Great Boat, by *Arthur Edmunds*

CHAPTER SIX
PROFESSIONAL ADVICE

The previous commentary concerns what to look for on your boat describes what becomes obvious to the experienced owner. But many of these areas of inspection need to be checked in greater detail. It is for this reason we turn to the professional surveyor of boats who has experience in finding problems with boat hulls. When the surveyor looks at many different hulls, he finds defects common to that particular type of hull material and construction. They may even know a particular model from a boat manufacturer and the experiences of other boat owners. Keep in mind a surveyor's job is to find defects, and he is not very popular with the seller of a boat. Who wants to hear from a wise guy inspector who is going to tell you what is wrong with a boat you really like and in which you have invested a large amount of money?

The professional surveyor may save you a great amount of money after you read the report of inspection. Isn't it worth a $250 fee to find out you are about to make a $25,000 or $250,000 mistake? A boat dealer won't be happy you have hired a surveyor to check out your new boat before delivery, but he does know the survey is a necessity your insurance company will require. Definitely, a survey report is vital for a used boat, no matter how good it looks. The insuror wants to know what type of risk it is taking when approving a casualty insurance policy. In this regard, they not only want to know the condition of the hull, interior, and engines, but they must have a list of all the installed equipment, especially electronics, so they can prudently insure against theft. It is important the surveyor see the boat out of the water so the hull can be properly inspected.

You may think you can check your boat as well as anyone, but you probably don't have the experience of looking at many different hulls. Surveying is often a matter of two heads being better than one. The professional often finds problems others overlook, or are too distracted to identify. It is important to be present while the surveyor is doing his job, not to constantly look over his shoulder, but to listen to his comments and ask pertinent questions. Basically, the surveyor is trained to look at a very small area, make a judgment of the material and the manner in which it is installed, and move on to a new section. For more information concerning surveys read, *Fiberglass Boat Survey*, by Arthur Edmunds, published by Bristol Fashion Publications, 1-800-478-7147.

You can find a surveyor by asking your insurance agent with whom he has worked. Look in the Yellow Pages, or ask your local boatyard. When you first contact a surveyor, ask about the fee for your particular boat and experience with that model. Often, a surveyor will not be familiar with sailboats and the rigging, and will not go up the mast to check the spreaders and the masthead. Be sure to tell the surveyor exactly what you want. Mention you plan to buy the boat, where you will be operating, and the name of your insurance agent. If you have any particular doubts about how something is put together, now is the time to ask. If the survey is prolonged, or if you have to wait for the boatyard to haul the boat, it might be very informative to take the surveyor to lunch and discuss what is happening in the world of boats.

The report of survey informs your insurance company of what they are insuring, informs you of present and potential problems on board, and may give you an idea of what repairs are required so you can get an estimate from the repair yard.

The surveyors will honestly list all defects they find, but they can only see what is there on the date of inspection. A bulkhead may later be found to have a loose glass fiber overlay to the hull which may, or may not, have been loose when the surveyor was on board. If a tank is empty, but is later found to have a leak, you could not have expected the surveyor to fill all the tanks -- at your expense -- to check for leaks. If a glass fiber hull has gel coat on the outside and is painted on the inside, it is impossible for the surveyor to see any laminate defects. An ultrasonic thickness tester may, or may not, detect any interior delamination.

ENGINE MECHANICS

You can't go anywhere without smooth running engines and it is usually difficult to get to the local repair yard when you most need them. When you consider buying a used boat, it is often money well spent to hire an experienced engine mechanic to run the engine with the boat in the water, even though he charges about fifty dollars per hour. The hull surveyors can usually see if the engine starts and runs smoothly, but they cannot be expected to know all of the preventive maintenance procedures and the signs of premature wear. The mechanic will have the test equipment to check all of the operating temperatures and pressures. When the engine is so important to your enjoyment of using the boat, it is a small expense to pay the mechanic to insure the equipment is in top condition.

While you have the mechanic on board, look at all the installed systems in the engineroom. After all, the engine spaces may contain one-third of the total value of the boat, and this equipment depreciates with wear. Certainly it is deserving of the best in inspection and maintenance. Don't overlook the exhaust system that must be gas tight throughout its length. The mechanic can tell you about proper maintenance procedures: when to change the engine oil and filters, when to change the impeller on the water pump, when to change the transmission oil filter, and when to clean or change the fuel filters. Like the mechanic you use for your car, he can provide a necessary service if he knows your engine and realizes you want to have the best care for your equipment.

ELECTRONIC TECHNICIANS

If you require a small boat for afternoon trips, you probably won't have much in the category of electronics, but even the smallest hulls may use a speedometer and depth finder. On larger hulls there may be many thousands invested in radar, communications gear, and safety electronics to the extent of one-quarter of the total boat value. New boats will have warranties to repair any defects, but used boats should be carefully investigated to see the operation is satisfactory. This can best be accomplished by hiring an electronics expert to check out every item.

The location of some types of electronics may cause interference with each other and with the magnetic compass. This is a situation where the technician can provide invaluable advice. Antennas must be located on the top of the deck house to provide good reception with little interference and the coaxial cable connecting the antenna to the transmitters must be of the proper size. It is an easy task to turn on a piece of electronics to see if it is operating, but it is another matter to check for accuracy. Is the speedometer giving a correct reading of knots? Is the fathometer accurate within two feet? Is the radar accurate within half a mile? Is the radio transmitter sending out peak power? All of these questions can be answered with the help of a good electronics technician, as he can make the necessary adjustments on the installed gear. Even the installation of the fathometer and the speedometer may profit from his advice. Magnetic influences from gear in the engineroom, or from a television set close to the connecting cable may adversely affect the accuracy of the readings.

It is both interesting and worthwhile to spend a few hours checking out the accuracy of your electronics. If you are about twenty to thirty miles from a US Coast Guard Station or a commercial marine operation, you can use the VHF radio to see if your signal strength is acceptable. You can drop a weighted line in the water less than ten feet deep, with the boat stopped. Measure the line length to the water when the line is vertical (a lead line) and check the fathometer accuracy. After all, we are only interested in the first six feet of depth, unless we are looking for a wreck or a school of fish. When you are a mile or two away from a point of land, a lighthouse, or a relatively straight section of coastline, you can stop the boat and accurately fix your position using three visual bearings. This can be compared with the radar range to see if it is accurate.

Speed determination is a lengthy and somewhat tedious process. This checks your electronics and gives you a permanent record of what speed to expect at a particular engine RPM. Usually, this must be accomplished in open water as we are not allowed to go full speed in the intracoastal waterways or in other protected waters. It is best to use a new nautical chart of your area and select two easily visible landmarks that are on the chart and which are a half mile to a mile and a half apart. Make sure you can run a straight course about a mile offshore that does not cross a rock or a shoal, and which has the two marks in sight.

Do not select a course between two buoys as they swing on their anchor chain and may be fifty yards away from their charted position. Also, there may be other boats in the vicinity of the buoys which makes a straight run impossible. Start your speed runs about a quarter mile away from the marks so you are at a constant speed and RPM when you pass the mark. Make the eight or ten speed runs when the sea is calm and the wind is less than five knots. Note the sweep second hand of your watch (or stopwatch) when the first mark is abeam (ninety degrees from your constant heading). Use a hand bearing compass to make sure the mark is exactly abeam. Continue on a straight course with constant RPM until the second mark is abeam and the time is noted in minutes and seconds. Normally, it is sufficient to make these speed runs at 1/3 RPM, 2/3 RPM, and at maximum allowable RPM. A graph can then be made and the speed interpolated for any RPM, for future reference.

Run each speed test in two directions and average the elapsed times, to cancel the effects of wind and current. If there is more than one knot difference in runs at the same RPM, the test should be repeated. The speed in knots is determined by dividing the distance between marks in nautical miles, by the elapsed time in hours. (Knots equals miles per hour.) Convert the seconds into minutes by dividing by sixty. Further convert the minutes into hours by dividing by sixty.

For example, if we time the run at three minutes and eighteen seconds, (0.055 hours), between marks that are 0.8 miles apart, speed is then 0.8 miles divided by 0.055 hours, which is 14.5 knots. One mile in one minute is sixty knots and one mile in three minutes is twenty knots. The modern method of speed measurement is with an electronic radar gun, but only if it has been properly calibrated.

SUMMARY

This chapter on professional advice explained the necessity for a second opinion on the condition of your boat, new or used. Many owners think they don't want the extra expense of a surveyor, but your insurance company will insist on a written report. The expense of having a mechanic look over the engine and all equipment in the engineroom not only affects your purchase but it gives you confidence in knowing exactly what is in top condition and what is in need of immediate repair. Your electronics deserve close attention to check their correct operation. We need all of the electronics when in an emergency or when trying to make port in a foggy or rainy night, and then is not the time to question their accuracy. Running speed tests between landmarks is a necessary procedure to check your speedometer readings and to have a permanent record of boat speed at various engine RPM.

    It is logical to follow the example of commercial ships when considering safety on boats. The U.S. Coast Guard inspects passenger carrying ships to see if they have the necessary safety equipment and to see that the crew are properly trained in emergency procedures. Most of the insurors require ships to be inspected by one of the classification societies such as American Bureau of Shipping or Lloyd's Register of Shipping. By the same reasoning, we need professional advice to help us locate any problems with our boats.

Buying a Great Boat, by Arthur Edmunds

CHAPTER SEVEN
NECESSARY EQUIPMENT

We are bombarded with advertisements for boat gear and it is hard to choose from the many types and manufacturers. Surprisingly, much of the equipment is eventually necessary for a large boat that does extensive ocean cruising. But a small boat under thirty feet may only need a few items. Actually, the gear you have on board is related to the area you frequent, no matter what the boat size. If you stay in the rivers, small lakes, and intracoastal waterways, you will need safety equipment, but not to the same extent as if you cruised the oceans. In this regard, we hasten to emphasize that the Great Lakes, Long Island Sound, Chesapeake Bay, and Delaware Bay are not protected waters.

Weather conditions drastically change the boating scene, of course, in any part of the country. During the Summer, we can cross from Florida to the Bahamas on flat calm water, but the same trip in the Winter may encounter twenty foot swells when the wind is from the North, blowing against the Northerly flowing Gulf Stream current. Even a sudden Summer thunderstorm can cause many accidents to boats and to owners who are not well prepared.

Every boat must have the equipment required for safety:

1. We need lifejackets (PFD) for each person, including small sizes for young people.

Buying a Great Boat, by Arthur Edmunds

2. Proper running lights even though you think you will not operate after sunset. An anchor light is also required.
3. A horn, bell, or whistle for operating in fog.
4. Fire extinguishers and emergency flares.
5. Anchors and one hundred feet of line.
6. Fenders and dock lines.
7. Magnetic Compass and charts.
8. Batteries for the electronics.
9. Boarding Ladder or stern swim platform.
10. Life raft or dinghy if going offshore.
11. Stanchions and lifelines around the deck.
12. Safety harnesses for the crew to wear and attach to the boat when moving about the deck in rough seas. The safe procedure to follow is not to fall overboard!

When considering electronics, there are many choices with all the latest upgrades and new features. If you are in protected waters, you made not need digital gear to distract you from enjoying the cruise. However, avid fishermen will probably have a fathometer. These depth finders can range from a basic measurement of water depth to a video presentation of the entire water column from the surface to the bottom, showing any fish movement in between.

If you travel in an area where ship channels converge, Radar is a reassuring safety factor, especially at night and in fog. Radar is a valuable navigation tool and can tell you when you are on a collision course, even in the worst of weather. Coastal cruising in rain or fog quickly shows the need.

Also necessary for coastal or offshore cruising is a reliable means of communication. Many people use cellular telephones, but they have to make sure the batteries are fully charged and they are within twenty miles of a relay antenna. VHF radios are commonly used in many different ratings of power output (watts). These are line of sight communications with a range of twenty to thirty miles, if the transmitting power is sufficient. Single sideband (SSB) radio transmitters are used for higher power and longer distances.

A brief explanation of line of sight communications may be helpful. All radio wave transmissions in the higher frequency range are limited in range because of the curvature of the earth. This includes Radar, VHF radio and television, cellular telephones. For the same reason, our vision is only to the horizon but increases greatly with our height above the surface. You may have looked out on the ocean and seen the masts and stack of a ship but were unable to see the hull clearly. The hull was below the horizon, but the taller masts were above the horizon. This is called seeing a ship hull down.

A very tall antenna will have a long range. An antenna ten feet above the water may send a signal 3.5 miles before it is at the horizon. If there is a ten foot tall antenna on a receiving boat, the signal may be heard at a distance of seven miles. A four hundred foot tall TV transmitting tower may send out a signal for 23 miles but the range will be increased by the height of the receiving antenna.

CRUISING EQUIPMENT IN THE PAST

A short look at boating in the past may serve to put the subject of equipment in proper perspective. Recent television and movie presentations of old ship sinkings have shown just how little the old ships and boats had available. Before World War I, communications were only by Morse code telegraphy and then only when a long wire antenna was fitted and there was an operator listening for a signal. Short distance voice radio soon followed. Radar and Sonar were not developed until World War II and they did not appear on recreational boats until much later. It is still common for small boats to operate in protected waters and coastwise within sight of land without any electronic gear and with only minimum slow speed power.

The use of electronics on small boats really became

prevalent after the development of the transistor in 1948 by three scientists at Bell Laboratories. Consumer, solid state electronics developed soon after with the use of printed circuit boards, integrated circuits, and eventually microchips. The weak point in all electronic circuits had been the glass vacuum tube, and these were fortunately eliminated. It is truly amazing to see the many advances in boat electronics in the past thirty years. There has been a great contribution to boating safety by the introduction of smaller, more reliable and affordable electronic equipment.

Many owners like to simplify their boating from the standpoint of investment and repair. Unless required for reasons of safety, you can enjoy boating without too much installed gear. Cooking on board is always a job no one wants and many still follow the old custom of heating soup, canned stew, and beans on a two-burner alcohol stove. An ice chest stays cool for two days, after which canned food becomes the only recourse. Some interesting menus can be made using canned or packaged foods that do not require refrigeration. When you have to stay alert on a boat for sixteen hours each day, having a light meal four times a day is usually preferable (7 AM - 11 AM - 3 PM - 7PM) to the alternative of eating too much three times daily. A large assortment of drinks can be found in cans and plastic bottles, and canned or dried fruit makes good snacks between meals or on a night watch.

OTHER EQUIPMENT

We have not mentioned some gear that is definitely considered by those who go offshore on rough waters. The degree of difficulty of an ocean trip is dependent on the sea conditions and not necessarily on the length of the voyage. The short trip from Los Angeles to Catalina Island (30 miles) may become rough at any time in the open ocean, but going from Miami to Bimini Island (60 miles) in the Summer usually is a flat calm crossing. Safety on the ocean calls for an Emergency Position Indicating Radio Beacon (EPIRB). This is a radio transmitter that sends out a signal on the aircraft emergency frequency when it is switched on. Aircraft can home in on this signal by taking bearings on their direction finder and thus locate the source. This is a worldwide system that has become a necessity. The self-contained battery must be replaced frequently to insure correct operation.

In addition, the modern system of navigation has become the Global Positioning System (GPS) because of the great convenience and simplicity of operation. By receiving signals from orbiting satellites, GPS shows your latitude and longitude. On some equipment, this position may be electronically combined with a video presentation of charts in your area so you can see your progress through channels and past buoys. New electronic navigation gear is being introduced every year.

All of this latest electronic means of navigation is excellent with judicious use in the proper situation. Do not expect it to be a cure-all. You should always have an alternative plan in case of gear failure. The most prevalent problem with all electronics is the failure of battery power, either self contained or from of the boat's house battery. Also, electronics will usually fail if the equipment gets wet. Always keep spare batteries and be able to start the engine with a separate battery in order to charge the house load battery.

Always keep in mind what you might do if the boat loses power to the communication and navigation gear. A good Dead Reckoning (DR) plot on a paper chart is invaluable for keeping track of where you have been and to suggest a future course. It may seem improbable, but oarlock sockets can easily be installed on a boat less than thirty feet to provide a safe trip home by rowing when there is a loss of engine power.

Buying a Great Boat, by Arthur Edmunds

KEEP YOUR TRIP SAFE

1. Always slow your speed if you see a boat to your right (starboard). You are required to let them pass ahead of you.

2. Stay out of ship channels. Assume all ships will not change course or stop, especially in the open ocean.

3. If you meet a boat head on, change your course to the right (starboard). The other boat should do the same, to his right.

4. If another boat overtakes you from astern, (he is moving faster) keep your course and speed and allow him to pass.

5. If you stand in one position and sight over a stanchion or fitting on your deck three or four times, you can see another boat's bearing moving to the right or to the left, or having no change in relative bearing. A hand bearing compass does a better job. When the bearing is unchanged, the danger of a collision exists. If the boat is on your port side, proceed with caution to make sure he slows to let you pass. If the other boat is on your starboard side, see Number One above, and slow your speed.

6. If you meet a boat that is fishing or SCUBA diving, slow your speed and turn away from their position. Their nets and divers may be some distance from their boat.

7. Sailboats have the right of way only when sailing, but they often get close calls from speeding powerboats. This is a dangerous practice as it keeps the powerboat operator's attention away from other boats and other dangers. As on the highways, speed kills.

8. When in rain or fog, slow to a minimum speed and listen for other fog horns. Sound your fog horn and use your radar. If inland, try to find a protected anchorage area to use temporarily, preferably in shallow water where deep draft boats will not enter.

9. Proceed slowly at night and constantly look for the lights of other boats. Observe the above procedures and take bearings of other boats to see if the danger of a collision exists.

10. Keep in mind the maritime General Prudential rule. The fact a collision occurred shows neither boat took sufficient action to prevent it.

11. When in a crowded waterway or a narrow entrance channel, keep to the right, just like on the highway. Don't hog the middle.

12. Get to know the lights and buoys in you area so they will be more familiar at night.

13. If you see another boat in need of help, stop and try to assist. If you can't provide help, at least radio to the US Coast Guard. A very small boat can slowly tow a vessel four times its length.

Buying a Great Boat, by Arthur Edmunds

Buying a Great Boat, by Arthur Edmunds

CHAPTER EIGHT
THE MOTIVATION FOR OWNING A BOAT

There are many reasons for buying a boat, all of which are very important to the owner, and they apply to both power and sail. A brief discussion of these reasons may help the buyer with his decision to buy.

THE TIME FACTOR

Most of us who are devoted to boats have been taught from an early age. We learned the responsibilities and maintenance required and the safe limits to which we can extend ourselves and the hull. The necessities of a working life and family responsibilities later become more important and put time restrictions on our boating life. Many find vacations are the only available time for boats and it has become very expensive to maintain a boat just for a week or two of use. This has fueled the great popularity of chartering in the Caribbean Islands or at home, in different boats and for any time period. Airline travel to these islands is usually not too difficult.

Time is also a factor in deciding between power and sail. Many people want to cruise as far as possible and they tire of sailing at five knots instead of ten or fifteen knots under power. On the other hand, people who race sailboats in a local club program like the competitive spirit of being with other boats for a few hours on a weekend afternoon. Whatever the decision, about eighty percent of the boats sold in the USA are powerboats, probably because of the restrictions of time.

TRADITION AND NOSTALGIA

Many people like to stay with the customs and heritage of their families, or region of the country. Their role models are the iron men and wooden ships that established the sea ports in the past centuries. These seamen of long ago established their trade, fishing, and ocean commerce with a minimum of investment in their boat and equipment. It is this return to the uncomplicated life that appeals to many boat owners. Cruising or sailing on the weekends provide a brief interlude of enjoyment of the waterways, just as our ancestors enjoyed their traditions of the sea.

Even with the modern trend to glass fiber hulls and decks, the shapes can be made to any modern or traditional style. The trim can be of varnished wood if the owner is willing to maintain the finish. The use of wood for a boat's interior depends on the owner's budget, as the joinerwork can be as modern or antique as necessary. The efficient interior arrangements, used fifty years ago, are still as popular and effective, particularly on sailboats. Most of the changes we see today are the result of planning for double beds and larger showers. Fuel and water tanks are also much larger than in past decades, probably because of higher speeds and more frequent showers.

THE SPORTS FACTOR

There is no doubt boats are sometimes only a vehicle to participate in another activity. Fishing has always been in the top ten of leisure sports. Every size and type of hull has been used for both inshore and offshore trolling, trawling, and long lining. From fifteen feet of boat upwards, fishermen all over the world try every stream, river and ocean to find a fresh dinner.

No less enthusiastic, the SCUBA divers are prevalent in any country, not so much for fishing, but for lost articles from any era. The development of the breathing regulator by Jacques Costeau and his subsequent films started an entire industry and an international sport. While inland cave diving and beach exploration are popular, most divers work from boats to look at the reefs and ocean bottom. Usually a semi-enclosed boat with a head is chosen. Lockers for wet suits and secure holders for air bottles are a necessity. It is not hard to fit out a boat for SCUBA, and any boatyard is able to make the necessary installations in most any type of hull.

Easy access to and from the boat is necessary on a SCUBA dive boat as the weight of the tank and size of the awkward swim fins present a problem in mobility. Many use a boat with a rubber side and has low freeboard, such as a rigid inflatable boat (RIB). The glass fiber hulls with a rubber tube at the sheer have become very popular both with divers and as rescue vessels. They are easy to roll out from and climb into from the water. Others simply take off the fins and tanks while in the water and then climb into the hull. There is no doubt a swim platform or ramp at the stern will provide the same ease of access to the boat.

THE STATUS SYMBOL

We all know of people who own businesses and influence clients by taking them on their boat to talk of future contracts. The idea of having a captive audience in a relaxing scene is very appealing to most entrepreneurs. Some people who have large, custom boats, keep buying and selling to attain a longer hull, which they think is impressive to their friends. A few have a new boat under construction before the first hull is launched. This may be the finest example of conspicuous consumption. Maybe we should be grateful to these large boat owners who provide work for everyone in the business of construction and repair of boats.

Others who seek to impress the public show off by tearing through crowded inland waterways at high speeds without any objective in mind. Apparently they think buying a boat with large engines and big fuel bills will gain the respect of their friends. It is usually the inexperienced owner who has never learned boating safety who attacks the water the way a stock car driver attacks the oval track. Not only fast powerboats try the intimidation act. All of us who have raced sailboats have seen status seekers at five knots, with mouths going at sixty knots, in a feeble attempt to push competition aside.

We all know of people who try to be associated with those of fame or wealth, hoping to be accepted in their social scene. Boats are one vehicle for movement in these circles. Some have boats, not for the joy of boating, but as a requirement for membership in a yacht club of famous members. Often, the boat may only leave the dock for a few days each year. The boat becomes a hideaway for parties and card games and to provide a climb up the social ladder.

THE DREAM MACHINE

All of us are influenced by stories we read in magazines and books. Who hasn't wondered about tropical islands and unfamiliar places when reading the pages of C.S. Forrester, The National Geographic magazine, Herman Melville, Jack London, and Richard Henry Dana? Many people turn to these tales and facts and think of having a boat to escape from their daily problems. They have hopes of sailing into the challenges of the sea and the pleasures of new experiences. People dream of going fishing for a living or possibly searching for old wrecks and lost treasures.

These dreams of a more relaxing existence motivate owners to cruise in their boats, whether it is for a few hours or for an extended vacation. It is the same casual thinking that encourages a land bound person to sit on the beach and gaze at the ocean. The boat owner may only have time for a short run on a river or bay, but they know in their subconscious a long trip is possible if the opportunity arises.

FAMILY FUN

Probably, the most dominant reason for owning a boat is to have family activities on the water. Picnics, swimming and fishing are perfect for holding family life together and they provide great enjoyment that will be remembered for many years. If the children are involved, they will learn the responsibilities of boating safety and how to perform the required maintenance. This is an opportunity to learn skills and valuable lessons that will be with them for a lifetime of enjoyable boating.

Boats are always a gathering place for friends and family. A boat owner is always popular with relatives as they all want to be invited for a short trip or a vacation. If a boat owner needs new acquaintances, he can just do some maintenance and be prepared to deal with the sudden appearance of people who want to start a conversation and who want to be invited aboard. A boat attracts new friends like honey attracts bears. There is no shortage of people who would like to be part of the crew in any type of boat.

Young people, and most adults, are fascinated with the educating experience when learning how to navigate on the ocean or lakes. The problems of determining your position and plotting on a chart provide many hours of great enjoyment.

Buying a Great Boat, by Arthur Edmunds

CHAPTER NINE
SAILBOATS

THE DAYSAILER

    This terminology covers a multitude of boats up to thirty-three feet in length, and is generally meant to be an open boat without berths or cooking facilities. There are always exceptions to any definition and some daysailers are used for carrying camping gear and tents used in secluded areas. Others put a cover over the boom and sleep on board on air mattresses. Both are really roughing it, as all the food must be in a portable ice chest.

    This type of sailboat is the least expensive as it has a completely open deck, with possibly a short, covered foredeck, and very little equipment. It is an excellent boat for gaining good sailing skills and having maximum fun. Most every experienced racing skipper will tell you they learned their basic sailing in very small boats. Sailboat racing in an identical fleet of small boats provides both enjoyment and competition.

    The daysailer may have ballast in a deep keel, ballast plus a centerboard, or just a centerboard without ballast. The advantage of a centerboard is the boat has very shallow draft and it can be put on a trailer or floated up to a beach. The disadvantage of the centerboard without ballast added is the boat will probably not be self righting and a capsize caused by a strong gust of wind will leave the mast submerged and the hull half full of water. In this situation, the crew must get in the water, push the boat upright, and bail the hull before climbing aboard and resuming sailing. All daysailers must have flotation material installed so the hull will not sink when full of water.

Some shallow keelboats may also be put on a trailer with a crane, and they may or may not be self righting, depending on the beam and amount of ballast. Normally, a keel sailboat is kept at an anchorage or at a dock, and the boat buyer should have the problem solved before buying. Daysailing catamarans usually have a centerboard but with no ballast, great care must be taken to shorten sail in strong winds to prevent a capsize. Catamarans are more difficult to turn upright after a capsize than monohulls. If an owner is not familiar with the details of keelboats, centerboard boats, monohulls and multihulls, it would be wise to take a sailing class or crew with other people to become familiar with all of the boats on the market.

CRUISING SAILBOATS

By obvious definition, cruising sailboats are larger and are fitted with berths, lockers, head, galley, an auxiliary engine, or means to install an outboard motor. Usually, twenty-five to forty percent of the total boat weight is lead ballast, depending on the length and beam of the hull. A centerboard may be designed into the boat if shallow draft is desired. Except in larger hulls, all of the accommodations are on one level, as low in the hull as possible. This lowers the center of gravity of the boat weight. A low center of gravity is desirable to keep the sailboat as upright as possible when it is heeled over by the force of the wind in the sails.

Cruising sailboats are slow speed, displacement type vessels and both forward and aft portions of the hull are narrow in shape in order to reduce resistance. They approach the shape of a canoe in the underbody. This narrow shape greatly reduces the interior room and load carrying capacity of a sailboat when compared with a powerboat of equal length.

The usable space in any hull is dependent on the length of the boat measured at the waterline (LWL), and not necessarily the overall length of the deck (LOA). Sailboats built before 1960 commonly had waterline lengths (LWL) ten to fifteen feet shorter than the length overall (LOA). The reason for this was the customary styling of previous years. It was also a holdover from the period when sailboats had long mainsail booms and bowsprits. The modern practice of having a shorter distance from the waterline ending to the bow lowers the weight at the ends of the hull and reduces the tendency to pitch into a seaway. These distances are called overhangs.

RIGGING

The stainless steel 1 x 19 wire rope rigging on a sailboat supports the mast, and the headstay (jibstay located at the bow) provides a place to attach the jib. Normally, there are eight pieces of rigging wire on a cruising sailboat; headstay, backstay, two upper shrouds, and four lower shrouds. The shrouds are located opposite the mast, port and starboard. The lower end of each wire at the deck has a turnbuckle (bottle screw in England) so the tension can be adjusted to keep the mast in a straight line when sailing. In order to allow some movement as the mast flexes slightly, each end of each rigging wire has a 'Y' shaped clevis.

When sailing close to the wind, the windward shrouds are under tension, while the leeward shrouds are slack. The shrouds are adjusted with the turnbuckles so the mainsail track on the aft side of the mast is straight when sailing on the wind. The turnbuckles are secured to the hull with stainless steel bars called chainplates. These go through the deck and are bolted to knees or to a bulkhead. The head stay and backstay chainplates are located outside the hull and are bolted through the hull material. The entire rigging assembly is held together with stainless steel pins retained with cotter pins. The ends of these cotter pins must be bent flat and covered with tape so sails and fingers are not cut.

The top of the mast has a masthead fitting to hold the upper end of the upper shrouds, headstay, backstay, and halyards. These halyards (or haul yards) raise the mainsail and the jibs to the top of the mast. The four lower shrouds are secured to the mast about half height. There are aluminum spreaders at this height secured to the mast and to the upper shrouds so the mast will not bend in the middle. Every part of the rigging is essential for safe operation.

Each part of the rigging should be checked annually for excessive wear or bending. Especially important are the end fittings where the wire rope has been swaged to the inside of a stainless steel tube that forms the attachment of the wire rope to the turnbuckle. Cracks may develop through these stainless steel tubes. The spreader attachment to the upper shrouds definitely has to be inspected as any failure of this fitting will cause the mast to collapse. Where the mast penetrates the deck, or cabin top, water leaks can be prevented by installing a waterproof material around the mast and securing it with stainless steel hose clamps or bands.

New sailboats are usually sold with the mast and rigging but without sails. Many different sailmakers can provide the usual sails made of Dacron. Other materials and new sailmaking technology may be used to decrease stretching, especially when applied to racing sails. Sails stuffed into bags occupy a great amount of space inside a boat, especially when you are trying to live aboard. New sails arrive folded in a manner similar to a road map and they occupy one-quarter of the space of a sail stuffed into a bag. It is not too difficult for two people to lay out the foot of a sail and fold it on top of itself in about eighteen inch folds. Three basic sails are on a cruising sailboat: the mainsail, a large jib, and a small jib. By contrast, a racing sailboat may have ten or more sails.

Buying a Great Boat, by Arthur Edmunds

    There are some fine products that make sail handling easier. These are primarily roller reefing for both the jib and the mainsail. They allow permanent storage of the sail on the headstay or on the boom. The sail can be rolled out to any particular area consistent with the existing wind strength. These items are expensive but do provide much easier sail handling when only two people operate the boat. Since the mast and sails are the prime method of propulsion, they must be inspected frequently and treated with care.

Buying a Great Boat, by Arthur Edmunds

CHAPTER TEN
AN ANATOMY OF BOAT COSTS

If you look at many boats at a boat show or in a dealer's showroom, it becomes obvious why there are price differences when comparing the same length of hull. Maybe the glass fiber hull and deck are the same, but the engines may be different, and the quality of the materials used on the hull interior may be unusual. Certainly, there is a large cost variance between a painted interior and one finished with plastic laminates or with varnished wood trim. All of the prices mentioned in this chapter are just average for manufactured boats of decent quality, and do not represent all of the boating industry. Certainly, custom built boats have prices that may be comparable or may be much higher in initial cost, depending on the type of boat and the builder.

Surprisingly, sailboats and powerboats of the same length are priced very closely together, but the sailboat cost does not include sails. The cost of large engines in powerboats offset the cost of mast, rigging, and ballast in a sailboat. There are many exceptions to this comparison, but we are discussing average prices only for the purpose of providing comparative information for the new boat buyer.

The following presentation of price comparisons represent a group of average boats. They have been taken from manufacturers' advertised prices noted at the time of publication.

Buying a Great Boat, by Arthur Edmunds

OVERALL LENGTH	PRICE RANGE
20	$18,000 - $29,000
25	$28,000 - $48,000
28	$40,000 - $68,000
30	$70,000 - $120,000
35	$120,000 - $168,000
40	$180,000 - $350,000

Approximate prices of new sailboats and powerboats.

ITEM	25 FT BOAT	35 FT BOAT
Hull and framing	6,000	22,500
Deck	5,000	23,000
Bulkheads	1,000	5,000
Rub rails and hand rails	500	3,500
One inboard engine and exhaust	6,000	13,500
Battery and electrical system	2,000	4,500
Shaft, strut and prop	1,000	3,500
Rudder and steering	1,000	3,500
Controls and instruments	1,000	3,500
Seats on deck	500	4,500
Deck hardware	500	2,500
Windshield and deck house	2,800	8,500
Berths	500	3,500
Head and shower	1,200	3,500
Galley	1,500	3,500
Dining table and seats	1,500	3,500
Lockers	1,000	2,500
Tanks and Piping	2,000	8,500
Interior trim and headliner	--------	6,500
Total	35,000	129,500

Approximate prices of new boat components.

We will attempt to analyze where the cost of a boat is distributed. All costs are estimated and vary widely with the size of the boat and the quality of materials. The costs stated in the tables should not be used for replacement estimates. The labor of installation after the boat has been built is much greater than the cost in a manufacturer's plant. All of the stated prices include the builder's overhead and profit.

REPLACEMENT OF COMPONENTS

CRACK IN THE HULL OR DECK

Sometimes, everyone has a bad day. They may approach the dock too fast and have the hull cracked when it hits a piling. Let's assume the damage is eighteen inches long and three inches wide. The boatyard will have to cut out the damaged laminate to solid glass fiber and taper the inside edge prior to laminating alternate layers of mat and woven roving with epoxy resin.

Just the laminating may take three days of labor plus materials. After the inside glass laminate, the exterior is filled with an epoxy resin putty and the gel coat is applied. This gel coat is covered with a plastic film while wet to assure a smooth, glossy finish. After curing, the repaired area is polished with rubbing compound and waxed. This outside finishing may take another twelve hours of labor.

It would not be unusual to have a repair bill of thirty-six hours at forty dollars per hour plus $185 material cost. The collision with the dock may cost a minimum of $1625 and possibly $500 more if some interior joinerwork has to be removed to gain access to the inside of the damaged area. Molding the hull initially is easy compared with the difficulty of later repairs at a boatyard.

This repair to a glass fiber hull is typical of damage anywhere on the hull or deck. An exception may be in areas where there is a core in the middle of two glass laminates. Any core will be damaged in a collision and some may have absorbed water to an area larger than the cracked glass laminate. In this case, the core will have to be removed to the point of finding completely dry material. Unless the repair is unusually large in area, the core is not usually replaced, and the damaged area is completely rebuilt with solid glass laminate.

REPLACEMENT OF A RADAR

Any electronics replacement is primarily concerned with the antenna and sensor installation. This is always more difficult than just bringing aboard a new black box. In the case of a radar, the cost ranges from $1500 to $3000 just for the components, when considering the average 12-mile radar range. In order to be compatible with the new transceiver, the antenna and coaxial cable will have to be replaced, also.

Possibly twenty hours may be necessary for the replacement, and the total installation costs may exceed $3500. Electronics components are always additional to the new boat price, and the owner should be cognizant of these costs when adding or replacing. Other electronics will involve similar costs, to a greater or lesser degree. Depending on the power of the transmitter, a communications radio may be half, or the same, as a radar installation.

INSTALLING A FATHOMETER

Prices vary widely with depth finders, as you may have a basic indicator of water depth or it may be a video presentation. The latter uses a screen of varying size that displays the water column to varying depths, depending on the output power at the transducer (the transmitter and receiver of sound signals). Usually, this video presentation is desired by people who fish in deep water, in an attempt to locate schools of fish below the surface.

The transducer may be located on the stern, just below the waterline, or it may be inside the hull. When inboard, it may have its own through hull fitting, or it may be in close contact with a smooth portion of a glass fiber hull, without a through hull fitting. The cost of a depth finder and installation may be as little as three hundred dollars or as much as $1500 dollars, depending on the manufacturer and the power output of the system.

INBOARD ENGINE REPAIR

Engines in a boat are almost like the engine in your car or truck, and you pay the same for parts and hourly rates. Each type of repair requires a different amount of time and you should receive an estimate prior to proceeding. It is always difficult to work on an engine in a boat as it is usually in a very cramped location. Access by hatches in the deck are necessary and these hatches must be supported by posts to take the load of walking on them.

If the engine has to be removed for replacement or major overhaul, there must be access to the top of the engine so a crane can lift it ashore. When there is a roof over the engine, there must be hatches in it also, or it may be removable.

The main engine uses sea water to cool the engine cooling water in most installations, and both circulate in a heat exchanger. It is common to have failure of the water pump or leaks inside the heat exchanger and both problems are detected by a rise in the engine temperature. This should be immediately repaired. If your surveyor notes an engine problem, you should get a repair estimate from the boatyard and the seller may deduct that cost from the agreed boat cost.

INSTALLING A BILGE PUMP

Pumps in each bilge area are a must to remove unwanted bilge water from a hull or piping leak. A glass fiber boat is normally absolutely watertight and we see problems only when the deck to hull joint, a hatch, a portlight, or a piping fitting is not properly installed. A pump should be installed between each pair of watertight bulkheads and in a small boat there are usually two bulkheads, just forward, and just aft of the engine space. This means three pumps are necessary; one aft, one forward, and one in the engine space.

It is an easy job for the owner to replace a bilge pump and they can be purchased for about $70. It may cost $125 to have a boatyard do the same job, but the piping to an overboard discharge through hull fitting may be somewhat more difficult. The pump should have a minimum capacity of 25 gallons per minute, and if a float switch is also installed, it should be wired to a warning light at the helm station. This warns the owner when a pump is operating for an extended period and is in danger of draining the boat's battery.

It is usually not necessary to cut another hole in the hull for a bilge pump discharge, as a T-fitting can be installed in the piping for a sink drain, deck drain, or a cockpit drain. Bilge pumps are often overlooked on a boat, but they are a life saver when there is water in the bilge. Some boats have used a 'T' fitting and valve in the sea water intake line for the inboard engine. This supplemental line leads to the bilge and can be used to pump the bilges in an emergency.

IMPROVE THE APPEARANCE OF YOUR BOAT

Owners hardly ever think of the boat's good looks after the day of purchase, but there are always some areas where improvements can be made. Too often, manufactured boats are made with white hulls and white (antique white) deck houses which leaves a very bland impression similar to a ghost in a snowstorm. Some of the outstanding glass fiber boats in the past have had light blue or light gray hulls with a red boot top stripe. See Figure 20. Hulls or decks made with many different colors may be ordered from a manufacturer, at extra cost, depending on the volume of their production. Of course, your hull can be painted by your boatyard with a polyurethane paint. Color schemes can be as plain or fancy as your imagination.

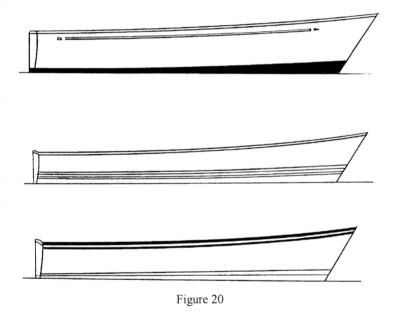

Figure 20

Just above the waterline, a single or double band can be painted at an angle to the waterline. This boot top will improve the appearance of most any hull. The bottom of the boot top may be the top of the antifouling bottom paint, or there may be an area of hull side color visible between the two. There are vinyl tapes available that can be used as a boot top instead of paint, but they must be applied on an absolutely clean surface, and they should be guaranteed not to loosen for two or three years. A stripe at the sheer may also be applied in the same manner, and the contrasting color greatly improves the hull appearance.

A teak or stainless steel pipe handrail secured to the side of a deck house not only improves safety, but the strong horizontal line will provide a better appearance. If you add a vinyl folding top or side curtains over part of the deck, make sure it is white in color. Other colors detract from the lines and shapes of the hull. In general, darker colors should be on the hull, closer to the waterline, and above the main deck the colors should be lighter. Costs for these changes assume the usual boatyard hourly fees plus materials, adding in the work performed by outside suppliers.

ADDING A THRUSTER

It is usual to install a bow or stern thruster on a boat less than forty feet in length, but they deserve mention as they are becoming very popular. Basically, they are six- to fifteen-inch diameter propellers driven by an electric or hydraulic motor. At the stern, they may be entirely aft of the transom, mounted on a bracket close to the boat's centerline. Alternately, the propeller is located below the waterline, aft of the transom, and the motor is just forward of the transom, inside the hull. Of course, there is a watertight seal at the hole in the stern and in both cases, there is a circular ring around the propeller to protect the blades from damage. Thrusters can be very valuable when docking with a strong wind blowing off of the dock.

The addition of a bow thruster is much more complicated and expensive. A glass fiber tube is installed from the port to starboard sides of the hull, about two feet below the waterline and four feet aft of the forefoot (The area where the stem meets the keel). This tube is about six inches larger than the propeller diameter and is overlaid with glass mat and woven roving to make it an integral, structural part of the hull. On centerline, the propeller is mounted at the top of the tube with a watertight seal to the inside of the hull where the motor is mounted. There must be sufficient glass overlay and framing on the inside of the hull to support the weight of the tube and thruster assembly.

It is only preference that determines whether you have a thruster located at the bow or at the stern, although the distance to the center of the waterline area, about which the boat turns, may be greater from the bow thruster location. One can also reason the stern of the boat turns from the rudder force, so it may be logical to have the thruster at the stern. Costs vary widely for the size of thruster and its location. Estimates from a boatyard are always necessary.

IS IT PRACTICAL TO LENGTHEN THE HULL

The question of making a longer hull from a shorter one is often asked, but not usually concerning a hull shorter than fifty feet in length. Mostly, an owner would like to have a fishing cockpit aft to make more recreational space. This addition has been accomplished many times by boat yards in any hull material and involves building a custom boat to exactly match the shape of the existing hull. On a glass fiber hull, twelve- to twenty-inch wide plywood planks are laid on the existing hull for a length of at least four feet and extending aft to the desired length. This plywood is supported with outside framing and must be a fair extension of the present hull. The plywood forms a rough molding surface for the new hull shape. The new construction of molded glass fiber to the existing hull thickness is supported with glass longitudinals and engine girder extensions that extend at least eight feet into the old hull. A new transom is molded to the new hull shape with solid glass laminate thicker than the old hull. The exterior is sanded and painted to match the existing hull.

The design, weights, and buoyancy of the hull extension must be carefully calculated by an experienced yacht designer to make sure the added weight of the extension, plus all equipment, is equal to the added buoyancy, to keep the boat in trim. In addition, the rudders, propellers, struts, shafts, shaft tubes, and exhausts will have to be relocated. The engine mounts are changed as the shaft angle will be less than before. The entire process is very expensive and may cost well over $55,000. The alternative, of course, is to look for a longer boat.

Some owners have read articles about the lengthening of ships by cutting in the middle and adding a new section. They ask whether this can be done with recreational yachts. Ships add length to get more cargo space, and with the same engine, they have only a small reduction in cruising speed. It is much more difficult to make this added length on a yacht as there is a large difference in design and construction.

Most ships are designed with constant sections amidships and tapering sections at the bow and stern. These midships sections may comprise thirty percent of the hull length. They are all identical with flat sides and a flat bottom, and with a constant radius at the bilge. The added length on a ship is also flat sided and with all constant sections to match.

The smaller yacht hull does not have constant sections and the hull is a shape of entirely compound curvature. Cutting a boat in the middle and adding a new length has been accomplished, but with a very large expenditure of money and man hours. Of course, the interior joinerwork must be completely rebuilt. The procedure for doing this is similar to the addition at the stern, but with a very important addition. When the hull is cut in two pieces, it is vital the centerline planes of the forward and aft sections be perfectly aligned so the keel, chine, and sheer lines are in the correct location to be faired together.

This type of custom construction is very expensive as it is about the same amount of work as building a new hull. The space in the building yard is occupied for many months, and skilled workers are needed to ensure the new hull is perfectly fair with the existing bow and stern, in addition to having identical lines both port and starboard. It takes a very unusual hull and a special breed of owner to undertake a project of this magnitude and cost.

ADDING A FISHING TOWER

People who are avid fishermen like the visibility provided by a tower that puts a crew member ten to twenty feet higher than the main deck. You can usually see further and possibly identify schools of fish that are close to the surface. But the tower height produces two to three times the movement as on the main deck whenever the boat rolls. Often, extra steering and engine controls are located on the tower.

Welded aluminum pipe is used to construct the tower and each one is custom made to fit the main deck. The four legs must be bolted through the deck and there must be reinforcements under the deck to transmit the loads to the hull. Aluminum angles under the deck are bolted to a bulkhead or to a glass fiber knee and to the aluminum backing plate under each leg of the tower. The towers may cost between $5000 and $10,000 and are usually installed on boats longer than thirty-six feet. Installation will vary with the type of deck arrangement.

The high weights of the tower and crew reduce the stability of the boat and the tower should be vacated when the boat is traveling in the trough of ocean waves. Only two people should use the tower at one time. Lookout platforms were used on the old sailing ships, but the most extreme example of a tower may have been the old swordfishing boats near the Straits Of Messina in the Mediterranean Sea. Many were about forty foot hulls with sixty foot masts and twenty feet of bowsprit and sternsprit. The sprits were necessary to secure the rigging that supported the mast.

ADDING A STERN PLATFORM

We mentioned earlier the value of a stern platform for getting aboard after swimming or for retrieving an injured person. It is an important addition if there is an inboard engine installation. Often, a stern platform cannot be installed if there are outboard motors or an inboard-outboard (stern drive) engine. At times, it may be practical to have just a permanent step installed of narrow width, just outboard of the engines.

The platform may be built from stainless steel pipe, welded to the shape of the transom and located a few inches above the exhaust outlets and usually nine to twelve inches above the waterline. Above the pipe the platform itself can be glass fiber or a teak grating, about 20 inches wide.

The framing, or brackets that support the platform, must be bolted through the transom, using backing plates inside the glass fiber hull. These supports should be spaced not more than four feet apart. Some boat yards prefer to use cast bronze brackets and some like stainless steel pipe with welded flanges as a base. If the platform itself is glass fiber, it can be bolted to the framing with flat head stainless steel bolts.

The cost involved is largely dependent on the beam of the boat and may be $400 on a small hull to over $8000 on a fifty foot boat. The cost will be substantially higher if a door is installed in the transom or if a stainless steel handrail is installed on the aft edge of the swim platform. They can be built as plain or as fancy as the owner's budget. Some large hulls have had hydraulically operated boarding platforms installed over the swim platform and extending under the aft deck. This can be accomplished at very high cost and usually only on large, custom hulls.

Buying a Great Boat, by Arthur Edmunds

CHAPTER ELEVEN
PROPELLERS

It may seem out of place to discuss propellers in a book concerning buying a hull, but this is one topic always mentioned by owners, and with deserved importance. Propellers always seem somewhat mysterious but everyone realizes they move the boat in an efficient manner if they have the correct number of blades and are of the correct size. We will confine this brief discussion to average recreational powerboats as there are many types of specialized propellers used for commercial, slow speed hulls, and for very high speed racing boats.

Propellers are always getting bent in too-shallow water and the repair yards are kept busy with replacements. On most boats, the propeller is deeper than the hull and is damaged very easily. To prevent this damage, there should be a short skeg or a long keel to protect the propeller, both of which can be installed after the boat has been built. The lowest point of the keel should be about six inches below the bottom tip of the propeller. In this manner, the keel may squeeze into the sand or mud before the propeller touches. Whether a skeg or keel is installed, the propeller shaft strut should be in the shape of a 'Y' so the lower leg provides some protection for the propeller.

PROPELLER FUNCTION

The purpose of the propeller is to convert the rotating

force (torsion) of the engine and shaft to thrust that moves the boat forward. This is accomplished by the lift produced at each propeller blade, which is curved in cross section. There is a definite high and low pressure side to each propeller blade, similar to the pressure distribution on an aircraft wing or propeller. There are many variables that influence propeller efficiency, and projections from the bottom of the hull are some of the worst offenders. They produce disturbed water flow and adversely affect propeller operation.

On inboard engine installations, there must be a shaft, strut, with a bearing, to support the propeller. These produce detrimental turbulent water, that are part of the losses experienced in the design of boats. In an attempt to reduce these losses, some unique and specialized propeller drive systems have been developed such as the Arneson surface drive and water jets, both of which use very different propellers.

In propeller design, many factors are taken into consideration, and one of the most important is limiting blade pressure to enhance efficiency. This is accomplished by having a large total blade area and a large diameter propeller, but not so large that the maximum engine rated RPM cannot be reached. You can't get the horsepower out of an engine if it cannot reach its rated RPM. A particular displacement hull requires a certain amount of thrust to move it efficiently, and a larger blade area means a lower blade pressure, as measured in pounds per square inch. This should not be interpreted to mean a greater number of wide blades, or a larger diameter are the prime factors to consider, as a number of other items enter into the decision for a propeller.

Experience with medium speed and fast recreational powerboats has been that three blades on propellers work efficiently on hulls to forty feet in length and four blades are used on longer hulls. Racing boats may have custom propellers of unusual design, while sailboats may use two bladed propellers to reduce resistance while sailing. Many sailboats or motorsailers on long cruises change to a three bladed propeller if they expect to be under power for a good part of the trip.

PROPELLER SIZE

Before the hull lines are drawn, the propeller diameter is determined so there is adequate clearance between the top of the propeller and the hull (twenty percent of diameter) and so the total area is sufficient for efficient operation. In order to arrive at a successful size propeller, the boat designer must take many factors into account, and finally decide on a reduction gear ratio that literally brings all of these items together. This ratio is the maximum engine rated RPM divided by the actual propeller RPM and may be 1.5:1, 2.0:1, or 2.5:1 in an average powerboat. For example, if the engine RPM maximum is 2800 RPM and there is a 2.0:1 reduction gear, the propeller would turn a maximum of 1400 RPM. The reduction gear is located in the same gear case as the reverse gear and is bolted to the engine just forward of the output shaft.

The propeller manufacturers publish charts of correct propeller diameters for various engine horsepower and revolutions per minute (RPM). These data should be followed without exception and the manufacturers should be consulted for each hull and engine combination. Your local propeller repair shop can provide these data. I emphasize we have been discussing a conventional inboard installation with shaft, strut, and rudder. If you have an inboard-outboard (I/O) stern drive or an outboard motor, you should purchase a propeller from the engine manufacturer and strictly follow the recommendations.

The propeller diameter on these stern mounted engines is strictly limited by the height of the cast housing and trim plate. Often, the propeller hub mounting is proprietary with each manufacturer, and substitute propellers are not interchangeable. Because of this limitation on diameter, there is usually not sufficient blade area to produce successful operation for larger hulls. This is why you don't see outboard motors used on cruising hulls over thirty feet in length. Exceptions do occur, and there have been some very lightweight racing hulls that have used four or six outboard motors. Other exceptions may include small boats in harbors or rivers that use outboard motors for pushing boats, logs, or barges at slow speeds for short periods of time, while making every attempt to reduce their cost of operation.

Propeller diameter can only be selected by carefully considering the engine horsepower, engine RPM, reduction gear, and whether the boat is a commercial fisherman or a lightweight recreational sport fisherman. The same engine may be used in both types of hulls, with a great difference in maximum speed. Propeller diameter may vary from twelve inches in a twenty-five foot boat to fifteen inches in a thirty foot hull, twenty inches in a thirty-five foot boat, to thirty inches in a sixty foot hull.

Propeller diameter is always selected first and is the most important size factor. Propeller pitch is then selected secondarily so the maximum engine RPM can be achieved. There has always been a great controversy about propeller pitch and it is a constant subject of comment among boat owners and yard workers. The prime misconception in these conversations is higher propeller pitch produces higher speed. Nothing could be further from the truth. Fast boats use higher pitch propellers than slower boats, but this is trying to compare two entirely different sets of facts without adequate reasoning. Pitch does not produce higher speed. It is only higher engine horsepower and lighter boat weight that produce higher speeds.

This misconception probably resulted from the naming of an invention, the screw propeller in 1844. Some people have misinterpreted this to mean the action of a screw moving in a solid block where a higher pitch screw moves further in the block than a smaller pitch screw, using the same driving force. It is a shame this erroneous thinking has persisted as the propeller inventor was truly a brilliant engineer. John Ericsson (1803-1889) was born in Sweden, but moved to London and then the USA. He became a US citizen in 1848 and was the designer of the famous boat MONITOR that had a propeller and a revolving gun turret when engaging the MERRIMACK in 1862. Before John Ericsson, all of the steamships used paddlewheels in one shape or another.

Pitch for the propeller of an average boat can be estimated from the formula:

Pitch in inches equals boat speed in knots multiplied by 1800 and divided by the propeller RPM.

$$P = KT \times 1800 / RPM$$

Propeller pitch for slow, displacement speed boats is twenty percent greater and propeller pitch on fast boats is twenty percent less.

For example, if a twenty knot boat has a propeller RPM of 1200, the correct pitch is 20 x 1800/1200, which equals thirty inches.

The reason for the variation of twenty percent from average to fast boats is the total efficiency is greater on fast hulls (less slip) . The total efficiency is less in slow boats (more slip) and thus the pitch has to be greater. The maximum propeller RPM is used in determining both diameter and pitch.

It is common for the ratio of propeller pitch to diameter to be 0.5 for displacement hulls. On moderate speed, average, hulls, this ratio can be 0.6 to 0.8. On planing hulls, the pitch to diameter ratio may be 0.9 to 1.2. It is good practice to check with the propeller manufacturer for each installation. When going on a long cruise, it is good to have a spare set of propellers on board, along with propeller nuts, cotter pins, and spare keys to fit the keyway on the propeller hub.

The aft end of the propeller shaft and the inside of the propeller hub are closely machined to the Society Of

Automotive Engineers (SAE) standard dimensions for shafts and keyways. A portion of the shaft and the inside of the propeller hub are tapered and each have a keyway to prevent the shaft from rotating on the propeller. After the taper, there is a straight, threaded section that takes a plain nut and a jamb nut, to keep the propeller from sliding aft. Aft of this threaded portion, there is a short stub of shaft with a hole in it for a cotter pin. Normally, the propeller, key, and nuts are silicon bronze, but the shaft is a precipitation hardened (PH) stainless steel alloy.

People with SCUBA gear can sometimes change propellers with the boat in the water, being very careful not to drop any of the parts. Propellers tend to get tightly stuck on the shaft taper, and a device called a propeller puller is a very useful product to have if you plan to do your own propeller replacement. *It* is better to plan any propeller repair or replacement at the same time you have the boat hauled for repainting of the bottom antifouling paint. It is always easier to check the condition of the underwater gear, replace the zincs, and replace the shaft bearing during the annual overhaul.

If you see spots of pink color on a bronze propeller, you will see they are pits where the zinc has been removed from the bronze alloy of copper, tin, and zinc. This is caused by stray electrical currents in the water and may sometimes be repaired by a propeller shop. Protection is provided by blocks of zinc located on the hull near the propeller, propeller shaft, struts, rudders, etc.

Buying a Great Boat, by Arthur Edmunds

CHAPTER TWELVE
THE BOATING MARKET

THE NEW BOAT DEALER

The boat dealer may represent many manufacturers or engine dealers, but they do business in a similar manner as the new car dealer. They depend on both service and repair to both hulls and engines in addition to selling new boats and equipment. They usually have an agreement with the boat manufacturers to sell a certain number of hulls each year and you may have a better chance at a discounted price during the Fall or Winter seasons.

If you stop at a boat dealer's location frequently, you may notice a particular model has been there for many months. If this boat fits your needs, the dealer may be anxious to sell it at a reduced price. Like any retail business, the dealer wants to sell his inventory as soon as possible. Sometimes, the dealer may not be able to reduce prices due to inventory loan commitments, but he may offer free dock space or oil changes for a short period of time as an incentive to purchase the boat.

The advantage of buying from a factory authorized dealer is primarily the warranty offered on new products they represent. However, some equipment bought for your boat may only have a warranty from the manufacturer and not necessarily from the boat dealer. It is wise to be a comparison shopper and investigate the hulls offered by many different boat dealers. If there is a boat show in your area, it always provides an opportunity to see exactly what is new on the boating scene. The manufacturers and dealers are usually very anxious to sell boats during the boat shows.

THE USED BOAT BROKERS

Boat brokers work in a similar manner to real estate brokers. They try to find the boat that will exactly fit your needs. Usually, they deal with boats over thirty-five feet, either from domestic or foreign custom builders or manufacturers. This means they are looking for a boat for a very selective buyer who has already seen what is being built by manufacturers and who wants something very different.

This does not mean the boat broker is indifferent to small boats. They are usually willing to talk with you about any type of hull and possibly suggest a dealer or a friend that may find what you want. The broker is always thinking you may become a client sometime in the future, or at least refer other boat buyers to his office. The broker will certainly try to locate a boat you want as he collects a fee from the seller equal to five or ten percent of the selling price.

USED BOATS
OTHER SOURCES

The used boat will not have a warranty on the hull or engine and it is absolutely necessary to hire a surveyor and engine mechanic to check both, no matter where you find the boat. You may read advertisements in the newspapers and boating magazines or you may hear of a boat from a friend. Whatever the source, find out all you can about the history of the hull, in addition to the survey. Try to talk with the boatyard manager where the boat was repaired and stored. This may be the most accurate source of information on the hull in question. The boatyard will normally be very helpful as they want to have you as a future customer.

Buying a Great Boat, by Arthur Edmunds

It is always good if you buy a boat from a friend when you know they have taken good maintenance procedures for many years. On the other hand, the friend may take offense if you say you want a professional survey before considering the hull. At the start of any discussion, it may be best to say the insurance company requires a survey and you will make the arrangements on a convenient date.

We have been talking about glass fiber hulls in this book as they are the most popular and possibly have the greatest longevity. Wood boats are difficult to sell as the maintenance is much higher, and you must really want to work on your boat, and have the necessary skills. Very old wood boats in reasonable condition are sometimes considered collector's items and are worthwhile restoring, but this is a very limited and specialized form of boat ownership. Aluminum hulls are very good and many large, custom, hulls are built of this material. You must be very careful to prevent corrosion on aluminum hulls from stray electrical currents in the water. There should be a hull potential meter, a 1:1 isolation transformer in the shore power, and many zinc blocks located on the keel.

Buying a Great Boat, by Arthur Edmunds

CHAPTER THIRTEEN
SITUATIONS THE OWNER WOULD RATHER FORGET

LOSS OF STEERING

The mechanical or hydraulic steering system sometimes has a failure which might be repaired with minimum delay. Otherwise, some means can be rigged to turn the rudder blade directly by securing lines to both sides of the rudder or lower unit housing of an outboard motor or stern drive. If you are really prepared, you could carry a steering oar that can be rigged on the transom in just such an emergency. It may seem laughable, but steering oars have been used for a thousand years.

If an inboard engine installation, there should always be provisions for an emergency tiller. The rudder post extends up to the main deck, with a square top machined on the post. When a deck plate is opened, a steel tiller arm can be set on the rudder post and the boat steered, with effort, from the main deck. With a twin engine installation, the boat can possibly be steered with one rudder, and with variations in engine RPM. Sometimes, a broken tie rod between the two rudders can be temporarily repaired using wood splints and the all-important baling wire.

Assuming an inboard rudder, the lazarette should be checked to insure all connections are secure and nothing has broken on the tiller (steering quadrant), tie rod between rudders, steering cables, or hydraulic cylinder. If there is a cable and sheave system or a push-pull cable, be certain everything is intact, especially the clamps that secure the cable to the hull.

If the rudder has dropped, the rudder collar and support plate has failed to take the weight of the rudder and the entire assembly must be rebuilt. It is wrong to allow the weight of the rudder to be borne by the stuffing box whose only purpose is to keep out water. If this is allowed to continue, the constant rudder movement will wear the packing in the stuffing box and water leaks will increase. A temporary repair may be made by tightly wrapping wire around the rudder post, inside the boat, and securing this wire to the deck beams. The loss of steering is a serious situation, especially when approaching a crowded docking space, and alternate procedures should be kept in mind.

This might be the best time to mention what to do in a panic situation with the loss of steering while approaching a dock. You don't want to hurt your boat, yourself, or anyone else, so you must stop all forward motion. Put the engine in reverse until you are stopped and then take time to reflect on the best solution. If you are about to be in close contact with other hulls, put over the fenders, and tie up to the other boat until you can be towed to the boatyard.

If you lose steering in open water, you might stop the engine, or reverse, or turn 180 degrees on a reverse course if you can turn with an engine. Sometimes the best option is to anchor until you can call for assistance, or attempt to make repairs. You will need a good assortment of tools to make your temporary repairs, and the following a just a short list of additional equipment for many situations.

Wood plugs for all through hull fittings
Collision Mat and Ropes
Rags for stuffing in cracks
Steering Oar

Underwater Epoxy Putty
Rowing Oars & Oarlocks
Cloth backed tape (Duct Tape)
Plastic Buckets (4)
Aluminum and Steel Wire
Tools for the Engine
1x2 and 2x4 wood; 6 FT long
Engine spare parts
Hand Drill and Bits
Boat Hook
Boarding Ladder
Three plastic flashlights
Dock and Anchor lines
Batteries in a plastic bag
Two or three anchors
First Aid Kit
Spare Compass
C.P.R. Airway
Radar Reflector
E.P.I.R.B.
Flares
V.H.F. radio

THEFT ON YOUR BOAT

If someone cuts your dock lines and tows your boat with another, there isn't much you can do to stop them, as this is an example of a professional theft where that particular boat is being taken specifically for resale in some foreign market. The thieves risk being seen by watchmen, bridgetenders, and by yard workers, especially in these days of high security marinas. There are some precautions you can take to minimize this event as it isn't too difficult to outwit a low life criminal.

The installation of a security system specifically designed for boats is always a good idea as the thief will turn away if sufficiently frightened or if they think the job has become too difficult. A good security system sounds an alarm at a watchman's office or at a police station, which cannot be heard on the boat, in addition to turning on a light and an alarm at the scene. The system can also be wired to open the starter switch on the boat so the engine cannot be run.

There is usually a main battery switch close to the batteries that selectively directs the alternator's charge to a certain bank of batteries. If this is turned to the OFF position when at the dock, it may discourage any thief to the point of leaving the scene. An additional switch in the starting circuit, plus the normal key switch, really confuses anyone who is not familiar with the boat. This switch can be hidden in a locker between the helm and the engineroom and will stop anyone from starting the engines unless they are a member of the crew.

When you leave the boat, turn off the fuel valves at the engineroom and at the tanks, wherever they are located. This will require a few extra minutes to start the engines for the next trip, but the security will be worthwhile. A thief will not want to spend the time to try and find the fuel valves and will leave before starting the engines.

Expensive electronics are often the target of boat thefts, but they can usually be bolted to their shelves at the time of installation. Anything you can do to make a theft more difficult will probably deter a thief. Criminals look for the easy way of stealing, without much effort and without much thought. Jewelry, cash, important papers, and portable items such as binoculars, GPS, cell phones, can be placed in a hidden safe that is bolted to a bulkhead inside a locker. There are literally hundreds of places to hide items on a boat. If you hide items in safes or lockers, make sure it is below the main deck, and probably below the cabin flooring. This confuses any thief as they will have to kneel on the floor to try to find any valuables. Trying to hide items on the bridge or in the main dining area makes it too easy to search, just like looking in a living room at home.

If a boat is kept on a trailer, all loose gear and valuables should be locked in the car or in a house. If you are leaving the boat for more than a few days, and the boat is in the driveway, you might jack up one wheel of the trailer to put it on blocks and remove one wheel. An outboard motor can be chained and locked to the trailer around the lower unit assembly. Also, the motor mounts can be chained and locked to the hull.

It is always money well spent to have a good insurance policy that covers the replacement cost of a boat when a theft occurs. Unfortunately, boats are seldom recovered after a theft, as they are quickly removed from the state and often out of the country to be easily sold for half their value. If a trailer is at a storage yard or at a marina, it is important to know there is twenty-four hour security that checks each boat and knows when a space or slip is supposed to be empty. People are often too busy to be on their boat every weekend, but the boat should be checked every few days for theft and for bilge water.

In today's world of identically manufactured boats, hull identification numbers on the transom and state registration numbers on the bow are sometimes the only distinction, in addition to the name of the boat. All of these are easily changed by a clever thief and it may be of some value, after a theft, for the owner to have some other distinguishing features. An owner might sand some part of the laminate on the glass hull before placing an unusual design, phrase, crest, or logo under a new glass laminate. This would make a permanent identification in the hull as the glass laminate is essentially translucent.

IS THE BOAT REALLY SEAWORTHY

The word seaworthy is a general term often used to

describe boats in advertising brochures. We can't really say any open boat, without a deck, is really seaworthy. It is hard to find a boat less than twenty-three feet in length you can really call seaworthy. All of the above hulls will take water over the bow when there are waves of two or three feet in height, and when it rains. Most boats will take water on the decks when in rough seas and especially when driven fast in choppy water. You will have to remove this water on deck, or in the hull, with a bucket and sponge. Beauty is in the eye of the beholder and seaworthiness is in the eye of the experienced sailor. It is a judgment call, and when efficiently operating a boat, you have to be very judgmental to be seaworthy. A large part of being seaworthy is not taking a boat into very rough waters.

Unusual wind strengths and wave heights will damage many ships, no matter how many oceans they have crossed. After every typhoon, hurricane or whole gale, boats and ships have been damaged or lost. Does this mean they were not seaworthy, or were the losses just unavoidable accidents?

If the hull laminate is adequate, if the deck to hull joint is watertight, and if there are stiffeners to prevent the hull from flexing, the hull is usually a quality product. If the deck or cabin side flex when you push on the laminate, it is usually a sign more stiffeners are required. Windows and hatches must be watertight, and a few short trips in rough water will make any leaks obvious. Everything about the hull must be designed and installed to resist the effects of fatigue and the repeated application of high loads, such as pounding into a seaway.

If the boat is used primarily on protected waters, rivers, and lakes, and is not used on rough waters, it will probably have a long life without any structural problems. However, if a powerboat is run at high speeds into five-foot waves, one might expect the forward areas to be stressed repeatedly to the point of glass fiber failure. These same areas may not be over stressed if operated at medium speeds.

It is easy to see, the longevity of any hull is greatly determined not only by the quality of construction, but by temperate operation in rough seas. Many recreational boats sit at the dock for extended periods and are used less than two hundred hours each year. Fiber glass boats will last a lifetime if they are used for only a few hours each season. The same general thinking applies to sailboats, as the experienced skipper will know when to reef the sails and change to a smaller jib as wind strength and wave height increase.

Safe operation of all types of boats is the key to both longevity and enjoyment. The owner must know the capabilities of his boat and crew and provide for prudent sailing in the weather conditions that exist. Many boat owners stay in the enjoyable waters of Biscayne Bay, Chesapeake Bay, Albemarle Sound, or Delaware Bay and they have as many memorable experiences as any other part of the USA. Boating gives many fine opportunities no matter where it is enjoyed.

THE BOAT SUNK AT THE DOCK

There are unfortunate accidents, even at the dock. A glass fiber hull had just had an air conditioning system installed where the condenser was water cooled with sea water. The heat exchanger was made of Monel tubing and there was a brass valve in the sea water line to the outside of the hull. No one was living on the boat when it sunk one night.

When the boat was pumped dry, the brass valve was found to be completely disintegrated. Apparently, there was an excessive amount of zinc in the brass alloy and there was galvanic corrosion with the Monel tubing. Brass and bronze alloys should not be used with those metals that are protected from corrosion (Carbon, Mercury, Monel, Inconel). In fact, none of these metals should be used with steel and aluminum. Bronze alloys, which are used for many items of marine hardware, can be used with passivated stainless steels and plastic fittings.

This situation with the air conditioning obviously did not follow the manufacturer's instructions. A plastic ball valve was probably the best solution for the problem. Certainly, there should be a valve on all through hull fittings, not only for repair and replacement, but in the event a fitting fails inboard of the hull surface. You can't be too careful when using different metals in the marine environment.

DON'T LOCATE TANKS IN THE STERN

Most small to medium size hulls have a small water tank in the bilge of the engineroom and have the fuel tanks outboard of the engine(s). This is a correct installation as the tanks are close to the middle of the boat and the trim of the boat is not changed when the tanks are full or empty. A problem arises when an owner wants greater fuel capacity for long cruising. The easy, and wrong, solution is to look at all the open space in the lazarette near the rudder, and conclude the tanks should be located aft.

If this is done, the trim of the boat will be permanently changed, the running attitude of the boat will be adversely affected. The exhaust will likely be under water, resulting in higher back pressure when starting.

If one or two tanks of small size, are located in the stern, they could be used during the first part of a long cruise and kept empty at all other times, thus limiting the deleterious effects of having the weight at the stern. Actually, the best, and most expensive, solution is to remove the existing tanks in the engineroom and replace them with wider and longer tanks in order to achieve the required capacity. There should be no fittings on the sides or bottom of any tank.

THE BOAT ROLLS EXCESSIVELY

We don't see many problems with rolling on boats less than thirty-five feet in length unless they have a fishing tower or other high weights installed. In fact, the main cause of excessive rolling in longer boats is there are too many weights located above the main deck. There seems to be a false impression among small boat builders that they can pile any amount of equipment on top of the main deck.

Careful attention should be given to the stability calculations for new motor yachts. There is a tendency to locate fishing towers, masts, cranes, small cars, boats, and motorcycles on the bridge deck above the main deck. All of this gear raises the center of gravity of the entire boat and makes the ride more uncomfortable for the passengers.

Some years ago, there was excessive rolling on a large motoryacht even in a small seas and a high center of gravity was suspected. When the boat was inspected, there were staterooms below the main deck forward of the engineroom. This was normal, but on the main deck there were many heavy carbon dioxide cylinders for the installed fire extinguisher system. There was also a large walk-in refrigerator and freezer along with the heavy compressors. In addition, a large hot water heater was also located on the main deck!

It was obvious all of this heavy equipment was misplaced and should have been located in the hull, just above the keel, and one stateroom should have been moved to the main deck. Corrections were recommended and outside ballast was added by welding to the steel hull. Aluminum angles can be welded to an aluminum hull and steel angles can be bolted through a glass fiber keel if ballast is necessary.

NO OPENING PORTS IN THE HULL SIDE

A motor yacht had opening portlights in the side of the hull, only twenty-four inches above the waterline, thus producing a very dangerous situation. It was careless to have these ports open when underway. Murphy's Law always produces unusual situations and this boat ran aground in a crowded river, heeling the hull over about seventy degrees. Water poured into the open portlights on one side. The hull filled with water and capsized.

After the SCUBA divers closed the portlights, the water was pumped out and a very costly rebuilding of the interior was started. The obvious question is why the opening ports were ever installed. The boat did not have fans for air circulation nor did it have air conditioning. Apparently, it had been thought the opening ports would bring in some fresh air, but with no regard for safety.

Air intakes above the main deck should be used for ventilation of the interior and especially the engineroom. Fans inside duct work can distribute the air to all compartments, and the traditional cowl ventilator can be used in many parts of the deck if forced air fans are not necessary.

GASOLINE ENGINE STALLING

I have has experienced unexpected gas engine stalling at slow to idle speeds after starting and running the engine without difficulty. These embarrassing events have occurred repeatedly on an engine that has been well maintained and with over five hundred hours of use, both with carburetor and with electronic fuel injection (EFI) engines. The engines usually restarted and ran well after two or three attempts.

Good mechanics have agreed the cause of stalling is probably fuel contaminated with both water and dirt. In the case of the carbureted engine it may also be a buildup of foreign deposits on the internal surfaces. In most cases, the carburetor must be removed and chemically cleaned before further use. Sometimes a periodic spray with a carburetor cleaner may be sufficient. The installation of an additional fuel filter and the use of premium grade fuel may also be necessary to assure clean operation.

The fuel injected gasoline engine is also afflicted with

problems if there is dirt or water in the fuel. A damaged fuel sensor may cause erratic running as well as clogged emission control valves. Fuel filters will ease the problems in many cases, and it may be necessary to use premium grade fuel with an additive in every tank of fuel for EFI engines.

EXHAUST INSTALLATIONS ON A V-DRIVE GAS ENGINE

We always learn from the mistakes that happen in the industry, and it is an unusual situation that often causes the mistake. Some years ago, an owner had a gas engine that was definitely not producing the rated horsepower. It was a V-drive installation where the exhaust came out of the forward portion of the engine block. The exhaust was an iron pipe that made a U-turn over the top of the engine and continued aft to the transom. This pipe was covered with insulation to keep it from burning the crew, until the cooling water was put into the exhaust.

Close inspection of the running engine revealed this iron exhaust pipe was within two inches of the row of spark plugs and some of the plugs were arcing to the exhaust pipe. Heavy duty rubber spark plug caps may have solved this problem, but the proper solution was to relocate the exhaust line to another location.

STAY AWAY FROM SHIPS

It seems people with small boats are fascinated with ships and like to steer close to them just to see what is happening. This is fine if the ship is at the dock, but it can be deadly if the ship is underway. Ships cannot maneuver quickly, especially in crowded channels, where they must stay on a prescribed course, as noted on the charts. Many ships are single engine and it often takes them two miles to stop from a slow speed of five knots.

It is very dangerous at night, as the ship may not see you on the radar, and may not be able to stop in any case. It is always prudent to stay out of ship channels at any time. The following are anecdotes of close encounters of the shipping kind that will serve to illustrate why boats and ships are kept completely separate, even though they use the same ocean. The small boat owner must keep alert and maneuver as necessary.

I was helping a friend sail a thirty-foot wood sailboat across the Gulf Of Mexico and 0200 found us plodding along in calm seas. Without any sound, light, or warning I was suddenly aware of the smell of diesel fuel and the unmistakable low hum of ventilation fans. I tacked immediately away from the odor and looked back only after getting the sails in proper order. It was an aircraft carrier that had no lights of any kind, and with no moon was barely discernible from a hundred yards away.

Apparently they were on night landing maneuvers and their radar could not pick up a small and close object. It took about three minutes for their patrol boats to locate us and blind us with large search lights. There was no conversation, and we sailed blindly along without further incident. It could have been a disaster if the carrier was underway.

Some time ago, a boat show was held at a commercial port facility, with a cargo ship moored just a few hundred yards away. On a busy show day with hundreds a people in attendance, the ship cleaned the outside of the boiler tubes (blew tubes) and deposited a heavy layer of black soot over all of the boat show and the attendees. This procedure involves blasting steam over the boiler tubes and is never allowed in any port in the world. Blowing tubes is only done when well at sea.

This event shows the disdain ship operators have for other people, whether in port or underway. Recent news events relating spilling of oil or garbage close to the beaches confirms the incompetence continues.

Several years ago, three USCG ships were traveling in a line in the open ocean, with about one mile between each ship. They were moving about ten knots and were being overtaken by a cargo ship traveling about sixteen knots. There was a twenty degree difference in courses between the cargo ship and the USCG cutters and the cargo ship crossed between two of the ships without changing course or speed.

This was a very dangerous situation where the cargo ship was required to keep clear as it was overtaking. There can be no excuse for this type of conduct at sea. Probably, the cargo ship was on autopilot and there was no one on the bridge. This is a common although unsafe practice.

IS YOUR BOAT SPEED WHAT YOU EXPECTED?

The modern, manufactured powerboat owner usually doesn't have any complaints about boat speed as they normally have large engines that produce more than adequate speed. Very few people question whether the boat is cruising at twenty or twenty-five knots. We discussed measuring boat speed in Chapter Six, and this section will emphasize the reasons your speed check may be faulty.

It is always good to check your installed speedometer, or at least have a chart of engine RPM that produces a particular boat speed. Make sure the measured mile is accurate and the electronic radar gun has been recently calibrated. When the boat is new and the engine is in top shape, you probably will find the best speeds attainable.

The following list shows what can be out of line when conducting a boat speed test, and are events that can easily happen:

1. Barnacles are on the hull bottom and propeller.

2. One or more of the propeller blades is bent or nicked.
3. The shaft bearing is worn to the point where the shaft is not rigid.
4. The boat is not in level trim.
5. The propeller may be the wrong size. Make sure you can achieve maximum rated engine RPM.
6. The engine may not have sufficient air for proper fuel combustion.
7. The fuel may be contaminated with dirt or water.
8. If gasoline, the spark plugs may be fouled.
9. The fuel filters may need replaced.

Always give yourself the best advantage when conducting a boat speed test. Go out in calm water with not more than a half load of fuel and water. Usually two people are sufficient for crew. It doesn't help boat speed to have a vinyl top or side curtains flapping in the breeze.

Probably just as important as boat speed is to know how much fuel is really in each tank and how far you can cruise at a moderate RPM with a certain amount of fuel. Electronic fuel gauges are often not accurate. Use a wood dipstick through the fill pipe to check the fuel level.

DON'T STOP UNLESS AN ELBOW STOPS YOU

We were on a pleasant cruise from Florida to the Bahamas when we encountered a twenty-three foot boat about twenty-five miles offshore. Two men were on board and apparently looking over their single engine. We asked if we could help or if they wanted a tow to shore. They said they were just fishing and they wouldn't need assistance. With this rebuff, we proceeded on our way, thinking this strange situation was something no experienced seaman would allow to happen.

It is doubtful a small boat would be fishing far offshore in the three knot Gulf Stream Current, as the fish are normally in shallow waters. Possibly, they were waiting for someone or something clandestine. Later, we thought we were fortunate to be relieved of any obligation to the small boat, as the ocean is sometimes not as friendly as it seems.

A few hours after this incident, the generator sounded a high temperature alarm. We didn't need the A.C. power to get to an anchorage, but the problem was immediately researched when the boat was comfortably secured. It was obvious the generator was not getting adequate cooling water and the question became the source of the mechanical problem.

The seacock at the through hull fitting and all the other valves were open and the sea water strainer was clear of any weeds or obstructions. The only recourse was to dismantle all the water inlet piping in the 130 degree engineroom. We finally found a reducing elbow fitting on the inlet side of the sea water filter was plugged with sea grass and not allowing water flow to the generator. This fitting was used to change the piping size to fit the sea water strainer.

The lesson to be learned from this experience is, reducing elbow fittings should not be used in any part of the sea water piping. If there are different piping sizes, straight reducing fittings, not elbows, may be used in the straight sections of piping. No mechanic, owner, or surveyor would catch this error in installation. Hopefully, the relating of this occurrence will alert owners and builders so the situation will not be repeated. The piping for the main engine, air conditioner, or watermaker could have the same problem.

WE ALL GO AGROUND

It is embarrassing and frustrating to be aground but it is a common occurrence most owners don't want to discuss. The author has been aground many times in the middle of a marked channel in the Intracoastal Waterway with a boat having five foot draft, and also aground many times on a boat with four foot draft. You have to be especially careful in Northern ports were there is a large difference in the heights of tides and the charts must be carefully analyzed in order to keep out of trouble.

Going aground at a high boat speed can be very dangerous to you and your crew no matter what the consistency of the bottom material. Obviously, if you hit a rock you may damage the hull, but you may only ooze to a stop if you go into mud or soft sand. It is not wise to use high boat speeds in waters where you may go aground. On Biscayne Bay, at South Miami, there is a notorious sand bank stretching completely across the bay, with only a narrow channel for access. The Featherbed Bank is deceiving in that the sand bar is not visible in most tidal changes and it has been the stopping point for many boats each year with bent propellers, rudders and propeller shafts.

When you do go aground, you put the engine in reverse and try to back off into deeper water. If the hull is aground over most of the length of the keel, you may have to try backing the boat with the rudder hard over. Another maneuver, is to heel the boat toward the deep water side by putting all the crew on one side of the deck. Sometimes this reduces the draft by an inch or two and the hull may be backed off the shoal.

If you are aground, in a small boat, in less than five feet of water, you might jump in the water and try to push the bow off by using your shoulder. Make sure you are attached to the boat with a line and have a boarding ladder set out so you can get aboard before the hull drifts away. When jumping in the water, always wear a pair of old sneakers as there could be glass or sharp rocks on the bottom. Pushing on an oar or long pole may also work.

When the above maneuvers don't get the hull free, you can take an anchor out in a dinghy to deep water (kedging) and try a strong pull on the anchor line. It helps to have a deck winch or an anchor windlass in this situation.

TRY NOT TO HIT THE DOCK

Every boat owner hits the dock or pilings now and then, and hopefully this is done at slow speed so no damage is done. People who are not familiar with boats need to gain experience in handling a boat in and out of the dock, no matter what their age. This experience can only be gained by practice over a period of many hours, preferably with a small boat less than thirty feet in length.

Usually, you can find an open dock, or set of pilings, away from the marina traffic where you can slowly and methodically approach the dock. It would be ideal if you can have the boat stopped, almost parallel to the dock, so you can reach out and drop a line on a dock cleat. Try to analyze each attempt so the next try will be an improvement.

Often, a harbor will have mooring buoys which may be used to practice landings when not occupied. Try to put your bow, or amidships portion, about two feet away from the buoy when the boat is completely stopped. If you hit the buoy, it is the same as hitting the dock. If there is a current in the area, or a fairly strong breeze, try to get the feel of how they affect the boat at slow speeds.

Having the ability to maneuver the boat around the docks in any wind or current is the essence of being an experienced owner. It is more difficult to get the boat tied to the dock when alone, but the fenders can be put out and the boat hook made ready long before the marina is approached. One of the finest deeds an owner can do is to take the younger generation on your boat and give them the opportunity to learn boat handling in and out of the docks.

Buying a Great Boat, by Arthur Edmunds

SUMMARY

The anecdotes in this chapter have been real events and are just a few of the problems an owner may encounter. They have been presented in an objective manner, hoping they will not be repeated. We all learn from the experiences and mistakes of the entire boating industry, which we hope will be very few in the future.

Buying a Great Boat, by Arthur Edmunds

APPENDIX ONE
LIST OF ILLUSTRATIONS

1. An Open Boat Type
2. A Type of Cruising Boat
3. The Semi-Enclosed Type of Hull
4. Types of Sailboats
5. A Cruising Catamaran
6. Boat Weight and Bare Hull Weight
7. A Stepped Hull Form
8. A Section of a Glass Fiber Boat
9. A Section of an Aluminum or Steel Hull
10. A Section of a Wood Hull
11. Engine Fuel Consumption Estimate
12. Engine Cost Approximation
13. Engine Horsepower and Boat Speed
14. Engines with a Normal and V-drive Installation
15. Engineroom Arrangement
16 - 16a. The Joint Where The Deck Meets The Hull
17. Head Arrangement
18. Galley Arrangement
19 - 19a. Interior Finish
20. Boot tops and sheer stripes

Buying a Great Boat, by Arthur Edmunds

APPENDIX TWO
INDEX

Add a longer hull	109
Aground	137
Air cushion vehicles	34
Air Intakes	71
Aluminum	39
Anchors	61
Ancient Boats	29
Antenna	76, 83
Appearance of the hull	106
Bare Hull	25
Berths	64
Bilge Pumps	105
Boarding Ladder	63
Boat Brokers	120
Boat Dealers	119
Boat Speed	50
Boat Types	15, 20
Boot Top	107
Cabin Sole	65
Capsized Sailboats	96
Catamarans	22
Chain for the Anchor	62
Chine Construction	32

Buying a Great Boat, by Arthur Edmunds

Cleats	61
Component Costs	102
Constant Bearing	86
Cooking	84
Corrosion	60
Cost of Boats	102
Cracks in the Hull	103
Cruising Boats	21, 64, 96
Daysailer	95
Deadrise	21
Deck	60
Deck to Hull Joint	58
Delamination	59
Developed Lines	40
Diameter, Propeller	115
Diesel Engines	48
Dishes	66
Displacement	32
Docking	62
Dead Reckoning Plot	85
Electronics	76, 82
Engine Cost	49
Engineroom	55, 69
Engine Stalling	132
Engines	45
EPIRB	84
Exhaust Installation	133
Ericsson, John	115
Fathometer	104
Finishes	67
Fishing Boats	20
Fishing Tower	111, 130
Frames, structural	60

Buying a Great Boat, by Arthur Edmunds

Fuel Consumption	47
Gaff Rigged	31
Galley	66
Galvanic Corrosion	129
Gasoline Engines	46
General Prudential Rule	86
Glass Fiber	25, 37
GPS	85
Heads	65
Helm	20
Heyerdahl, Thor	29
Hull Forms and shapes	21, 24
Hull Inspection	57, 73
Hydrofoils	33
Ice Chest	66, 84
Inboard/Outboard Drive (I/O)	51
Inspecting Your Boat	58
Insurance	74
Interiors	64
John Ericsson	115
Keel	60
Keelboats (Sailboats)	46
KON - TIKI	29
Laminates	25, 37
Lapstrake Construction	30
Line Of Sight	83
Longer Hull	109
Longevity	128
Mechanics	75
Model Tests	32

Buying a Great Boat, by Arthur Edmunds

Motivation of the Owner	89
Multihulls	22
Nostalgia	90
Number of Engines	49
Outboard Motors	47, 50
Pitch / Diameter Ratio	117
Pitch, Propeller	117
Portlights	71, 131
Prices Estimated	102
Propane	66
Propellers	52, 116
Radar	82, 104
Radio	82
Reducing Elbows	137
Reduction Gear	115
Refrigeration	66
Rigging	98
Rolling	130
Roller Reefing	98
Rub Rail	58
Runs To Check Speed	77
Safety Equipment	84
Safety Tips	85
Sailboat Types	19
Sails	98
SCUBA Boats	21
Seacock	69
Seaworthiness	127
Shaft, Propeller	118
Shaft RPM	45
Ships	133
Shower	65

Buying a Great Boat, by Arthur Edmunds

Shrouds	97
Speed	50, 77
Spreaders	98
Square Rigged Ships	31
Status Symbols	91
Steel Hulls	40
Steering	31, 123
Stepped Hulls	33
Stern Platform	111
Surface Drives	52
Surveyor	73
Tanks	130
Theft	125
Thrusters	108
Time Available for Boats	89
Tools	125
Torque	45
Traditions	90
Trailers	126
Trim of the Boat	130
Trimarans	24
Used Boats	120
VHF Radio	82
V - Drives	51
Ventilation	70
Water Jet Drive	53
Water Skiing	22
Watertight Compartment	70, 106
Windlass	62
Windows	70
Wood Construction	42
Zinc Anodes	39. 60

Buying a Great Boat, by Arthur Edmunds

APPENDIX THREE
TOOLS & SUPPLIES

This list has been compiled through the joint effort of our staff and many contributing writers.

As you delve deeper into boating, you will always find a need for one more tool, or a few more supplies. It is truly a case of "Too much is never enough and enough is always too much." With this in mind it is best to adapt the following to your boat's needs and storage capacity.

The boat tools should not be shared with the car or the home. Purchase a good quality plastic tool box larger than the current need. Remove the handle which will certainly come off when you are transferring the box to the boat or the dock. A second box for less used tools is also a good idea.

* Tools for a small cruising sailboat without electrical or plumbing systems.

** Tools to add to the list for a mid-sized cruiser with electrical, plumbing, electronics and an inboard engine.

*** Tools for the long-term cruiser or liveaboard sailor intending to make most of the repairs to most of the systems.

The balance of the list will be needed at your land base for extensive repairs, renovations, upgrades and restoration projects.

Buying a Great Boat, by Arthur Edmunds

HAND TOOLS

Good brands will carry a life time warranty.
* # 1, #2, #3 Phillips screwdrivers.
* Thin blade 3/16", medium blade 1/4", heavy blade 3/8" straight screwdrivers.
All the above should also be purchased in the stubby length.
** Jewelers set of screwdrivers.
** Various square drivers if you have this type of fastener on your boat. You will have to know the sizes you will need.
* Linesman pliers.
** Dikes/side cutters.
** Wire strippers. Buy the type with the stripper portion before the hinge.
** Terminal crimps.
** Digital multi-meter.
* Long-nose pliers.
** Needle-nose pliers.
* Vise Grips
* Small slip joint pliers (opens to 2").
*** Straight blade sheet metal cutters.
** Caulk gun.
*** Lufkin folding rule with brass slide extension.
** Large and small metal files.
* Set of allen wrenches 1/16" to 7/16" minimum.
*** China bristles paint brushes with an angle cut, in sizes 1", 1-1/2", 2", 2-1/2".
** School pencils.
** Pencil sharpener.
** Thin blade awl.
* 8" & 12" adjustable wrench.
** 12" Lenox hacksaw with 18, 24, & 32 teeth per inch blades.
** Estwing leather handle straight claw hammer.
*** A #2, & #3 nail set.

Buying a Great Boat, by Arthur Edmunds

** Combination wrench set.
** 1/4" drive socket set.
* 3/8" drive socket set.
** Ignition wrench set.
The term "set" is used because most of these tools are sold in sets. You can purchase them individually but you will spend more than buying a set.
** 24" to 36" adjustable wrench. The size will depend on the prop nut size of your boat.
** Battery carrying strap.
** Feeler gauges (blade type).
** Cordless drill with two batteries, charger, cobalt drill bits ranging from 1/32" to 3/8" and screwdriver bits with a good holder. These should be the same size as your hand screwdrivers.
** Large slip joint pliers (opens to 4").
*** 2# Ballpeen hammer.
Caulking iron.
*** Rubber mallet.
*** Small & large Wonder bars.
*** Diston small dovetail saw.
*** Diston coping saw.
*** Diston 13 point hand saw.
*** Stanley 25' tape measure.
*** Stanley combination square.
*** Stanley #40 wood chisels 1/2", 3/4", 1".
*** Block plane.
*** Half round wood file/rasp.
*** Heavy blade awl.
*** Larger size drill bits 7/16" to 1" forsener bits are the best for large wood bits. Metal bits should be cobalt.
*** Brad point bits 1/16" to 3/8".
Plug cutters 3/8" to 3/4"
*** Hole saw set.
*** Metal chisel and drift set.
** Right angle-straight and Phillips screwdrivers.

** Fish tape.
** Heavy gauge terminal crimp tool.
** Line wrench set.
** 1/2" drive socket set.
** Deep well socket set for all the different size drives you now own. Some of these may have been included when you purchased the sets.
*** 1/2" Breaker bar.
*** 1/2" Click stop torque wrench.
** 1/2" drive large sockets for all the bolts/nuts which are larger than the sets contain.
** Wrenches for the same bolts/nuts.

POWER TOOLS

Purchase brand name, heavy duty, commercial grade tools with a high ampere draw. These are the only tools that will last.
3/8" & 1/2" power drills.
Circular saw with good carbide tooth blades.
*** Random orbiting sander with 5" & 6" pads. Buy your 3M gold sanding disk in the 6" size and cut them down when you need the 5" size. Buy rolls of these grits. 60, 80, 100, 120, 150, 180.
Power miter box with an 80 tooth carbide blade.
3" x 24" or 4" x 24" belt sander. Buy at least three belts of each of these grits. 36, 80, 100, 120.
*** Soldering gun with electrical solder and flux.
Heat gun.
*** Random orbit buffer if you own a fiberglass boat.
Scrolling jigsaw with various wood and metal blades.
Router with various bits purchased as the jobs warrant. Always use roller bearing bits where applicable.
*** Sawz-all with various size and types of blades for wood/metal.

Buying a Great Boat, by Arthur Edmunds

Biscuit jointer with at least two hundred of the two larger size biscuits.
*** 25', 50', & 75' #12 wire extension cords.
Table or radial arm saw. The radial arm saw can be set up with a multitude of attachments to handle many different functions other than cross cutting and ripping.

SUPPLIES
All Stainless Steel Fasteners

** At least 50 each of these Phillips head screws.
#4 x 1/2", 3/4", 1" Flat and oval head.
#6 x 1/2", 3/4", 1", 1-1/4", 1-1/2", 1-3/4", 2" Flat and oval head.
#8, #10, #12 Same as #6 plus 2-1/2", 3" Flat and oval head.
** Finish washers for each of the above size screw numbers.
#6, #8, #10, 1/2", 3/4", 1", 1-1/2" Pan head.
** At least 10 each of these fasteners.
1/4" x 20 x 2", 3", 4" Flat and stove head bolts with 2 washers and 1 nut each.
5/16" & 3/8" x 1", 1-1/2", 2", 2-1/2", 3" machine bolts with 2 washers and 1 nut each.
** Cap nuts for each of the above sizes.
*** 1/4" x 2", 3", 4", 5" lag bolts with washers.
** Large fender washers for each of the above sizes.
*** 2 pieces of solid rod 3' long in 1/4", 3/8", 1/2".
*** 2 pieces of threaded rod 3' long with 6 nuts and washers per piece in 1/4", 3/8", 1/2".
* Various size cotter pins to replace ones which will need to be removed. Check the sizes you need before ordering or purchase a cotter pin kit with various sizes included.
18 gauge brass or stainless steel brads in 1/2", 3/4", 1"

ELECTRICAL

** Butt terminals, male and female quick disconnect terminals. Order at least 50 each for wire gauges, 22-18, 16-14, 12-10, 8.
** Spade connectors, stud connectors. Order at least 50 each for the same gauge of wire above to fit around stud sizes 4-6, 8-10, 1/4", 5/16", 3/8".
*** 10 terminals for each size battery cable in use on your boat.
** 6 battery clamps (lugs, the kind used on your car) with stud. Do not connect the battery wires directly to the clamp; use the stud and terminals.
** 200 each of 6" & 11" medium duty wire ties.
*** 100 each of 3/4" and 1-1/2" cable clamps.
*** 1 each 4, 6, 8, 10 position terminal blocks. 6 each 20 amp in-line fuse holders with 5 each of, 5 amp, 10 amp, 15 amp, & 20 amp fuses.
*** 100 ft each of wire gauges 18, 16, 14, 12, 10, 8. Tinned marine primary wire.
*** 25 ft each of wire gauges 6 & 4.
*** 10 butt connectors for 6 & 4 wire.
*** 10 ft of battery cable for each size you have in use on board.
*** 2 ft each of heat shrink tubing 3/16", 1/4", 3/8", 1/2," 3/4".

MISC. ELECTRICAL SUPPLIES

** Liquid electrical tape.
** Vinyl electrical tape.
** Nylon string to use as a wire fishing device.
** 1 Pair of battery jumper cables. They must be long enough to reach between the banks of batteries you may need to jump. If you can not find them this long, make up your own with heavy ends and # 2 battery cable.

** Jumper wires for testing. These can be made with 4 alligator clips and 12 gauge wire.
** 1 breaker or fuse holder for each different size and type you on have board.
** 1 fuse for each specialty fuse on board.
** 1 switch for each type on board.
** 2 extra bulbs for each type on board.
** 1 lamp socket for each type on board.
*** 1 of each shore line end or an extra 50' shore line set.
** 1 connector for each type of electronic instrument connector on board.

SEALANTS, PAINT AND REPAIR PRODUCTS

** 1 tube each of Teak Deck Systems, 3M 5200 in white, GE silicone in white & clear, Star Bright polysulfide underwater sealant, Sea Repair.
** 1 small kit each of Epoxy, Marine Tex, Boat Yard fiberglass with 6 oz. cloth and matching gel coat colors.
*** 1 qt each of varnish, top sides paint for each color on board, stain, paint thinner, acetone, lacquer thinner, Penatrol, boiled linseed oil.
*** Coffee cans.
*** Plastic pots in 1 qt size.
*** Disposable brushes in 1/2", 1", 1-1/2", 2", 2-1/2".

PLUMBING PARTS

* The best method of determining your needs for plumbing will be to go through your supply and waste systems measuring each hose, clamp, tubing and fitting type and size. With this list in hand purchase at least two of each type of fitting, 10 of each size clamp, hose to replace the longest

length of each size or fittings and hose to patch in the very long lengths. As with your shore power line, carry an extra water supply hose of no less than 50'. Also purchase water hose repair ends.

** This may not be considered plumbing by some, but it carries water, therefore it is included in this section. Your engines have many small sizes and lengths of hoses. As with the plumbing hoses, buy enough to replace the longest length of each size with the proper size clamps. These should be the heavy wall hose with wire reinforcement.

** If you have large exhaust lines you do not need to carry a full length. Do carry a large coffee can with 4 hose clamps which are a larger size than the exhaust hose. You must carry at least one spare impeller or a rebuilding kit with the impeller included for every pump on board. THIS IS A MUST!

MISC. SUPPLIES

* Shock cords and ends.
* Buckets.
* Sponges.
* Chamois.
** Toilet brush.
** Scrub brush.
** Deck brush with handle.
*** Roller handle, pan and pads.
** Bronze wool.
** Bronze scrub brush.
** Detergents.
** Cleaning products.
** Polishes.
** Compounds.
** Water resistant/proof glue.
*** Extension cord ends.

** Patching material for every inflatable on board.
** Repair parts for engine(s).
*** Antifreeze.
** Oils.
** Grease gun with grease.
** Transmission fluid.
* 5 gals of extra fuel.
* Duct tape.
* Riggers tape.
*** Masking tape.
*** Sheet sand paper in grits 50, 80, 100, 120, 150, 180, 220. At least 5 sheets of each grit.
* At least two complete sets of dock lines and anchor rodes.
* One 3/4" line (regardless of boat size to 45') three times the length of the boat. (Tow line)

Buying a Great Boat, by Arthur Edmunds

APPENDIX FOUR
GLOSSARY

This glossary has been compiled through a joint effort of the staff of Bristol Fashion Publications and many authors. It is not intended to cover the many thousands of words and terms in the language exclusive to boating. The longer you are around boats and boaters, the more of this language you will learn.

A

Accumulator tank - A tank used to add air pressure to the freshwater system thus reducing water pump run time.
Aft - Near the stern.
Amidships - Midway between the bow and the stern.
Antifouling - Bottom paint used to prevent growth on the boat bottom.
Athwartships - Any line running at a right angle to the fore/aft centerline.

B

Backer plate- Metal plate used to increase the strength of a through bolt application, such as with the installation of a cleat.
Ballast - Weight added to improve a boat's sea handling abilities of the boat or to counterbalance an unevenly

Buying a Great Boat, by Arthur Edmunds

loaded boat.

Beam - The widest point of the boat.

Bilge - The lowest point inside a boat.

Bilge pump - Underwater water pump used to remove water from the bilge.

Binnacle - A box or stand used to hold the compass.

Bolt - Any fastener with any head style and machine thread shank.

Boot stripe - Contrasting trim paint of a contrasting color located just above the bottom paint on the hull sides.

Breaker - Replaces a fuse to interrupt power on an electrical circuit when that circuit becomes overloaded or shorted.

Bridge - The steering station of a boat.

Brightwork - Polished metal or varnished wood aboard a boat.

Bristol Fashion - The highest standard of condition any vessel can obtain and the highest state of crew seamanship. The publishing company that brought you this book.

Bulkhead - A wall running across (athwartships) the boat.

Butt connectors - A type of crimp connector used to join two wires end to end in a continuing run of the wire.

C

Canvas - A general term used to describe cloth used for boat coverings. A type of cloth material.

Carlin - A structural beam joining the inboard ends of deck beams that are cut short around a mast or hatch.

Cavitation - Reduced propeller efficiency due to vapor pockets in areas of low pressure on the blades. Turbulence caused by prop rotation that reduces the efficiency of the prop.

Centerboard - A hinged board or plate at the bottom of a sailboat of shallow draft. It reduces leeway under sail.

Chafing gear - Any material used to prevent the abrasion of another material.

Chain - Equally sized inter-looping oblong rings commonly used for anchor rode.
Chain locker - A forward area of the vessel used for chain storage.
Chine - The intersection of the hull side with the hull bottom, usually in a moderate-speed to fast hull. Sailboats and displacement-speed powerboats usually have a round bilge and do not have a chine. Also, the turn of the hull below the waterline on each side of the boat. A sailboat hull, displacement hull and semi-displacement hull have a round chine. Planing hulls all have a hard (sharp corner) chine.
Chock - A metal fitting used in mooring or rigging to control the turn of the lines.
Cleat - A device used to secure a line aboard a vessel or on a dock.
Clevis - A Y-shaped piece of sailboat hardware about two to four inches long that connects a wire rope rigging terminal to one end of a turnbuckle.
Coaming - A barrier around the cockpit of a vessel to prevent water from washing into the cockpit.
Cockpit - Usually refers to the steering area of a sailboat or the fishing area of a sport-fishing boat. The sole of this area is always lower than the deck.
Companionway - An entrance into a boat or a stairway from one level of a boat's interior to another.
Cribbing - Large blocks of wood used to support the boat's hull during it's time on land.
Cutlass Bearing® - A rubber tube that is sized to a propeller shaft and fits inside the propeller shaft strut.

D

Davit - Generally used to describe a lifting device for a dinghy.
Delaminate - A term used to describe two or more layers of

any adhered material that have separated from each other because of moisture or air pockets in the laminate.

Device - A term used in conjunction with electrical systems. Generally used to describe lights, switches receptacles, etc.

Dinghy - Small boat used as a tender to the mother ship.

Displacement - The amount of water, in weight, displaced by the boat when floating.

Displacement Hull - A hull that has a wave crest at bow and stern and settles in the wave trough in the middle. A boat supported by its own ability to float while underway.

Dock - Any land based structure used for mooring a boat.

Draft - The distance from the waterline to the keel bottom. The amount of space (water) a boat needs between its waterline and the bottom of the body of water. When a boat's draft is greater than the water depth, you are aground.

Dry rot - This is not a true term as the decay of wood actually occurs in moist conditions.

F

Fairing - The process of smoothing a portion of the boat so it will present a very even and smooth surface after the finish is applied.

Fairing compound - The material used to achieve the fairing process.

Fairlead - A portion of rigging used to turn a line, cable or chain to increase the radius of the turn and thereby reduce friction.

Fall - The portion of a block and tackle system that moves up or down.

Fastening - Generally used to describe a means by which the planking is attached to the boat structure. Also used to describe screws, rivets, bolts, nails etc. (fastener)

Fiberglass - Clothlike material made from glass fibers and used with resin and hardener to increase the resin strength.

Filter - Any device used to filter impurities from any liquid or air.

Fin keel - A keel design that often resembles an up-side-down "T" when viewed from fore or aft.

Flame arrestor - A safety device placed on top of a gasoline carburetor to stop the flame flash of a backfiring engine.

Flat head - A screw head style that can be made flush with or recessed into the wood surface.

Float switch - An electrical switch commonly used to automatically control the on-off of a bilge pump. When this device is used, the pump is considered to be an automatic bilge pump.

Flying bridge - A steering station high above the deck level of the boat.

Fore - The front of a boat.

Fore-and-aft - A line running parallel to the keel. The keel runs fore-and-aft.

Forecastle - The area below decks in the forwardmost section. (pronunciation is often fo'c's'le)

Foredeck - The front deck.

Forward - Any position in front of amidships.

Freeboard - The distance on the hull from the waterline to the deck level.

Full keel - A keel design with heavy lead ballast and deep draft. This keel runs from the bow, to the stern at the rudder.

G

Galley - Kitchen.

Gelcoat - A hard, shiny coat over a fiberglass laminate that keeps water from the structural laminate.
Gimbals - A method of supporting anything that must remain level regardless of the boat's attitude.
Grommet - A ring pressed into a piece of cloth through which a line can be run.
Gross tonnage - The total interior space of a boat.
Ground tackle - Refers to the anchor, chain, line and connections as one unit.

H

Hanging locker - A closet with a rod for hanging clothes.
Hatch - An opening with a lid that open in an upward direction.
Hauling - Removing the boat from the water. The act of pulling on a line or rode is also called hauling.
Hawsehole - A hull opening for mooring lines or anchor rodes.
Hawsepipes - A pipe through the hull, for mooring or anchor rodes.
Head - Toilet. Also refers to the entire area of the bathroom.
Helm - The steering station and steering gear.
Holding tank - Used to hold waste for disposal ashore.
Hose - Any flexible tube capable of carrying a liquid.
Hull - The structure of a vessel not including any component other than the shell.
Hull lines - The drawing of the hull shape in plan, profile and sections (body plan).

I

Inboard - Positioned toward the center of the boat. An engine mounted inside the boat.

K

Keel - A downward protrusion running fore and aft on the center line of any boat's bottom. It is the main structural member.
King plank - The plank on the center line of a wooden laid deck.
Knees - A structural member reinforcing and connecting two other structural members. Also, two or more vertical beams at the bow of a tugboat used to push barges.

L

Launch - To put a boat into the water.
Lazarette - A storage compartment in the stern of a boat.
Lead - The material used for ballast.
Limber holes - Holes in the bilge timbers to allow water to run to the lowest part of the bilge, where it can be pumped out.
LOA - Length Over All. The over all length of a boat.
Locker - A storage area.
Log - A tube or cylinder through which a shaft or rudder stock runs from the inside to the outside. The log will have a packing gland (stuffing box) on the inside of the boat. Speed log is used to measure distance traveled. A book used to a keep record of the events on board a boat.
LWL - Length on the Waterline. The length of a boat at the water line.

M

Manifold - A group of valves connected by piping to tanks to allow filling and removal from one or more tanks.
Marine gear - Boat's transmission.
Mast - An upward pointing timber used as the sail's main support. Also used on power and sailboats to mount

flags, antennas and lights.
Mile - A statute mile (land mile) is 5280 feet. A nautical mile (water mile) or knot is 6080.2 feet.
Mizzen mast - The aftermost mast on a sailboat.

N

Nautical mile - A distance of 6080.2 feet
Navigation lights - Lights required to be in operation while underway at night. The lighting pattern varies with the type, size and use of the vessel.
Nut - A threaded six-sided device used in conjunction with a bolt.
Nylon - A material used for lines when some give is desirable. Hard nylon is used for plumbing and rigging fittings.

O

Oval head - A screw head used when the head can only be partially recessed. The raised (oval) portion of the head will remain above the surface.
Overhangs - The length from the bow or stern ending of the waterline to the forward or aft end of the hull.

P

Painter - A line used to tow or secure a small boat or dinghy.
Pan head - A screw head with a flat surface, used when the head will remain completely above the surface.
Panel - A term used to describe the main electrical distribution point, usually containing the breakers or fuses.
Pier - Same general use as a dock.
Pile - A concrete or wooden post driven or otherwise embedded into the water's bottom.
Piling - A multiple structure of piles.
Pipe - A rigid, thick-walled tube.

Planing hull - A hull design, which under sufficient speed, will rise above it's dead-in-the-water position and seem to ride on the water.

Planking - The covering members of a wooden structure.

Plug - A type of pipe, tubing or hose fitting. Describes any device used to stop water from entering the boat through the hull. A cylindrical piece of wood placed in a screw hole to hide the head of the screw.

Port - A land area for landing a boat. The left side when facing forward.

Propeller (Prop, Wheel, Screw) - Located at the end of the shaft. The prop must have at least two blades and propels the vessel through the water with a screwing motion.

R

Radar - A electronic instrument which can be used to "see" objects as blips on a display screen.

Rail - A nonstructural safety member on deck used as a banister to help prevent falling overboard.

Reduction gear - The gear inside the transmission housing that reduces the engine rpm to a propeller shaft Rpm that is optimum for that hull and engine.

Ribs - Another term for frames. The planking is fastened to these structural members.

Rigging - Generally refers to any item placed on the boat after the delivery of the vessel from the manufacturer. Also refers to all the wire rope, line, blocks, falls and other hardware needed for sail control.

Ring terminals - A crimp connector with a ring that can have a screw placed inside the ring for a secure connection.

Rode - Anchor line or chain.

Rope - A term that refers to cordage and this term is only used only on land. When any piece of cordage is on board a boat, it is referred to as line or one of it's more designating descriptions.

Round head - A screw or bolt head with a round surface that remains completely above the material being fastened.

Rudder - Located directly behind the prop and used to control the steering.

Rudder stock - Also known as rudder post. A piece of round, solid metal attached to the rudder at one end and the steering quadrant at the other.

S

Samson post - A large piece of material extending from the keel upward through the deck and used to secure lines for mooring or anchoring.

Screw - A threaded fastener. A term for propeller.

Screw thread - A loosely spaced, coarse thread used for wood and sheet metal screws.

Sea cock - A valve used to control the flow of water from the sea to the device it is supplying.

Shackle - A metal link with a pin to close the opening. Commonly used to secure the anchor to the rode.

Shaft - A solid metal cylinder that runs from the marine gear to the prop. The prop is mounted on the end of the shaft.

Shear pin - A small metal pin that inserted through the shaft and propeller on small boats. If the prop hits a hard object, the pin will "shear" without causing severe damage to the shaft.

Sheaves - The rolling wheel in a pulley.

Sheet metal screw - Any fastener that has a fully threaded shank of wood screw threads.

Ship - Any seagoing vessel. To ship an item on a boat means to bring it aboard.

Shock cord - An elastic line used to dampen the shock stress of a load.

Slip - A docking space for a boat. A berth.
Sole - The cabin and cockpit floor.
Spade rudder - A rudder that is not supported at its bottom.
Stability - The ability of a hull to return to level trim after being heeled by the forces of wind or water.
Stanchion - A metal post that holds the lifelines or railing along the deck's edge.
Starboard - The right side when facing forward.
Statute mile - A land mile. 5280 feet.
Stem - The forwardmost structural member of the hull.
Step - The base of the mast where the mast is let into the keel or mounted on the keel in a plate assembly.
Stern - The back .
Strut - A metal supporting device for the shaft.
Stuffing box -T he interior end of the log where packing is inserted to prevent water intrusion from the shaft or rudder stock.
Surveyor - A person who inspects the boat for integrity and safety.
Switch - Any device, except breakers, that interrupts the flow of electrical current to a device.

T

Tachometer - A instrument used to count the revolutions of anything turning, usually the engine, marine gear or shaft.
Tack rag - A rag with a sticky surface used to remove dust before applying a finish to any surface.
Tank - Any large container that holds a liquid.
Tapered plug - A wooden dowel tapered to a blunt point and is inserted into a seacock or hole in the hull in an emergency.
Tender - A small boat (dinghy) used to travel between shore and the mother ship. A boat with limited stability is said to be tender.

Terminal lugs - Car-style, battery cable ends.
Through hull (Thru hull) - Any fitting between the sea and the boat that goes "through" the hull material.
Tinned wire - Stranded copper wire with a tin additive to prevent corrosion.
Topsides - Refers to being on deck. The part above the waterline.
Torque (or Torsion) - The rotating force on a shaft. (lb-in)
Transmission - Refers to a marine or reduction gear.
Transom - The flat part of the stern.
Trim - The attitude with which the vessel floats or moves through the water.
Trip line - A small line made fast to the anchor crown. When weighing anchor this line is pulled to back the anchor out and thus release the anchor's hold in the bottom.
Tubing - A thin-walled metal or plastic cylinder, similar to pipe but having thinner walls.
Turn of the bilge - A term used to refer to the corner of the hull where the vertical hull sides meet the horizontal hull bottom.
Turnbuckles - In England, they are called bottle screws. They secure the wire rope rigging to the hull and are used to adjust the tension in the wire rope.

V

Valves - Any device that controls the flow of a liquid.
Vessel - A boat or ship.
VHF radio - The electronic radio used for short-range (10 to 20 mile maximum) communications between shore and vessels and between vessels.

W

Wake - The movement of water as a result of a vessel's movement through the water.

Washer - A flat, round piece of metal with a hole in the center. A washer is used to increase the holding power of a bolt and nut by distributing the stress over a larger area.

Waste pump - Any device used to pump waste.

Waterline - The line created at the intersection of the vessel's hull and the water's surface. A horizontal plane through a hull that defines the shape on the hull lines. The actual waterline or just waterline, is the height at that the boat floats. If weight is added to the boat, it floats at a deeper waterline.

Water pump - Any device used to pump water.

Wheel - Another term for prop or the steering wheel.

Whipping - Any method used, except a knot, to prevent a line end from unraveling.

Winch - A device used to pull in or let out line or rode. It is used to decrease the physical exertion needed to do the same task by hand.

Windlass - A type of winch used strictly with anchor rode.

Woodscrew - A fastener with only two-thirds of the shank threaded with a screw thread.

Y

Yacht - A term used to describe a pleasure boat, generally over twenty-five feet. Usually used to impress someone.

Yard - A place where boats are stored and repaired.

Z

Zebra mussel - A small, freshwater mussel that will clog anything in a short period of time.

Buying a Great Boat, by Arthur Edmunds

Buying a Great Boat, by Arthur Edmunds

Books published by
Bristol Fashion Publications
Free catalog, phone 1-800-478-7147

Boat Repair Made Easy — Haul Out
Written By John P. Kaufman

Boat Repair Made Easy — Finishes
Written By John P. Kaufman

Boat Repair Made Easy — Systems
Written By John P. Kaufman

Boat Repair Made Easy — Engines
Written By John P. Kaufman

Standard Ship's Log
Designed By John P. Kaufman

Large Ship's Log
Designed By John P. Kaufman

Custom Ship's Log
Designed By John P. Kaufman

Designing Power & Sail
Written By Arthur Edmunds

Fiberglass Boat Survey
Written By Arthur Edmunds

Building A Fiberglass Boat
Written By Arthur Edmunds

Buying A Great Boat
Written By Arthur Edmunds

Outfitting & Organizing Your Boat For A Day, A Week or A Lifetime
Written By Michael L. Frankel

Boater's Book of Nautical Terms
Written By David S. Yetman

Modern Boatworks
Written By David S. Yetman

Practical Seamanship
Written By David S. Yetman

Captain Jack's Basic Navigation
Written By Jack I. Davis

Captain Jack's Celestial Navigation
Written By Jack I. Davis

Captain Jack's Complete Navigation
Written By Jack I. Davis

Southwinds Gourmet
Written By Susan Garrett Mason

The Cruising Sailor
Written By Tom Dove

Daddy & I Go Boating
Written By Ken Kreisler

Buying a Great Boat, by Arthur Edmunds

My Grandpa Is A Tugboat Captain
Written By Ken Kreisler

Billy The Oysterman
Written By Ken Kreisler

Creating Comfort Afloat
Written By Janet Groene

Living Aboard
Written By Janet Groene

Simple Boat Projects
Written By Donald Boone

Racing The Ice To Cape Horn
Written By Frank Guernsey & Cy Zoerner

Boater's Checklist
Written By Clay Kelley

Florida Through The Islands
What Boaters Need To Know
Written By Captain Clay Kelley & Marybeth

Marine Weather Forecasting
Written By J. Frank Brumbaugh

Basic Boat Maintenance
Written By J. Frank Brumbaugh

Complete Guide To Gasoline Marine Engines
Written By John Fleming

Complete Guide To Outboard Engines
Written By John Fleming

Buying a Great Boat, by Arthur Edmunds

Complete Guide To Diesel Marine Engines
Written By John Fleming

Trouble Shooting Gasoline Marine Engines
Written By John Fleming

Trailer Boats
Written By Alex Zidock

Skipper's Handbook
Written By Robert S. Grossman

Wake Up & Water Ski
Written By Kimberly P. Robinson

White Squall - The Last Voyage Of Albatross
Written By Richard E. Langford

**Cruising South
What to Expect Along The ICW**
Written By Joan Healy

Electronics Aboard
Written By Stephen Fishman

**A Whale At the Port Quarter
A Treasure Chest of Sea Stories**
Written By Charles Gnaegy

**Five Against The Sea
A True Story of Courage & Survival**
Written By Ron Arias

Buying a Great Boat, by Arthur Edmunds

Scuttlebutt
Seafaring History & Lore
Written By Captain John Guest USCG Ret.

Cruising The South Pacific
Written By Douglas Austin

After Forty Years
How To Avoid The Pitfalls of Boating
Written By David Wheeler

VHF Marine Radio Handbook
Written By Mike Whitehead

Catch of The Day
How To Catch, Clean & Cook It
Written By Carla Johnson

Buying a Great Boat, by Arthur Edmunds